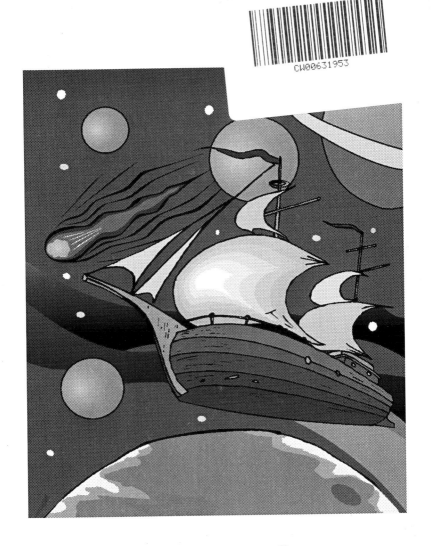

2001: A POETRY ODYSSEY CHESHIRE

Edited by Simon Harwin

To Auntie belle,
take a look at page 193

Luv your god-daughter
Dawn

First published in Great Britain in 2001 by
YOUNG WRITERS
Remus House,
Coltsfoot Drive,
Peterborough, PE2 9JX
Telephone (01733) 890066

HB ISBN 0 75432 986 0
SB ISBN 0 75432 987 9

FOREWORD

Young Writers was established in 1991 with the aim to promote creative writing in children, to make reading and writing poetry fun.

This year the 2001: A Poetry Odyssey competition again proved to be a tremendous success with over 50,000 entries received nationwide.

The amount of hard work and effort put into each entry impressed us all, and is reflective of the teaching skills in schools today.

The task of selecting poems for publication was a difficult one but nevertheless, an enjoyable experience. We hope you are as pleased with the final selection in *2001: A Poetry Odyssey Cheshire* as we are.

CONTENTS

Bankfield High School

Jacob Howden	1
Aeden McGuffie	2
Sean Andrews	2
Ben Hickton	3
Robin Farrington	4
Kimberley Littler	5
Sophie Bowman	5
Martin Jackson	6
Tom Beattie	6
Rebecca Naylor	7
Natalie Russell	8
Kayleigh Snelson	8
Julia Giblin	9
Craig Leech	10
Amy Burns	10
Amy Connor	11
Paul Kitching	12
Mark Duckett	12
Lauren Gee	13
Jessica Mercer	13
Louise McNabb	14
Johnnie Padilla	14
Anna Kilgariff	15
Johnathan Harrison	16
Ashley Hulse	17
Kerry-Ann Baynton	17
Yvonne Morris	18
Alison Lea	18
Andrew Mines	19
Adam Jackson	19
Lucy Downham	20
Karen Shaw	21
Hayden Lee	21
Beth Hughes	22
Stephanie Chester	22

Thomas McGauley	23
William Buckley	24
Alicia Ann Dunning	24
Neil Devany	25
Adele Mew	26
David Tickle	26
Luke Jackson	27
Michael Wilson	27
Danielle Buckley	28
Daniel Whitfield	28
Joe Fitzsimon	29
Emma Prendergast	30
Andrew Robinson	31
Alison Leadbetter	32
Michelle Richards	33
Jenny McGauley	34
Dawn Mason	35
Iain McConnell	36
Danny Roberts	37
Keith Schofield	38
Rebecca O'Connor	39
Sarah Lister	40
Stephen Bounds	41
Phil Woodward	42
Carolyn Henry	43
Claire Swift	44
Claire Campbell	45
Lisa Vickerstaffe	46
Jennifer Middleton	47
Kieran McCarthy	48
Lisa Anne Gatcliffe	48
Nathan Murphy	49
Anna Marie Bredin	49
David Woolfall	50
Gary Stevenson	50
Kelly Myler	51
Kirsty Hunter	51
Nicole Carter	52

Daniel Jones 53
Jessica Hunt 54

Cloughwood School
Andrew Goodier 55
Graham White 55
William Huxley 56
Jonathan Riley 56
Simon Ward 57
Matthew Pleavin 58
Nick Blezard 58
Philip Cooper 59
Gareth Lewis 60
Philip Martin 60
Leslie Rennie 61
Michael Lord Griffiths 62

Congleton High School
James Byrne 62
Jemma Armitage 63
Joseph Swindells 64
Nicola Beard 65
Alysa-Jayne Thomas 66
Susan Bossons 66
Gemma Comer 67
Andrew Scott 68
Claire Davis 68
Charlotte Barlow 69
Lucy Harding 70
Lucy Hodgkinson 71
Laura Butler 72
Alex Bourner 73
Laura Edwards 74
Benjamin Hadwick 75

Golborne High School
Alison Humphries 76
Clare Mills 76

Kayleigh Prior	77
Claire Singleton	78
Chris Hide	78
Emma Prior	79
Laura Mayoh	80
Catherine Stonier	81
Janine Lawton	82
Keith Gibson	83
Louise Northey	84
Mark O'Brien	85
Naomi Allen	86
Scott Tither	87
Craig Thompson	88
Lauren Foster	89
Kyle Simm	90
Rachel Grimshaw	90
Joshua Felton	91
Jenna Rutter	92
Hannah Lowe	93
Sarah Wilde	94
Lisa Quinn	95
Sarah Griffiths	96
Elizabeth Riley	96
Melissa Richards	97

Hartford High School

Natasha Evans	98
Hollie Lunn-Smith	98
Andy Oakes	99
Emily Merriman	100
Melissa Catherine Humphries	100
Dasha Beynon	101
Daniel Dobell	101
Catherine Davenport	102
Garreth Davies	102
Laura Mercer	103
Heather Greenwood	103
Nicola Buckley	104

Ben Walton	104
Ben Ditchburn	105
Vanessa Cooper	105
Daniel Sutton	106
Jamie Comley	106
Alison Telford	107
Gemma Dutton	107
Jamie Glaze	108
Rebecca Smith	108
Ben Aucamp	108
Syd Blake	109
Andrew Smith	109
Jade Wilkinson	109
Matthew Didsbury	110
Craig Thomson	110
Claire Bagnall	111
Josh Stokes	111
Caroline Scott	112
Tom Lightfoot	112
Andrew Timmis	113
Jonnie Crawshaw	113
Tom Mitchell	114
Emma Collinge	114
Tiffany Beattie	114
Holly Moncrieff	115
Kirsty Eyres	115
Mark Brown	116
Joseph Haslehurst	117
Laura Fuller	118
Anna Palfreyman	118
Kelly Thompson	119
Elliott Baron	119
Alex Rashid	120
Zoe Quilty	120
Eilidh McCallum	121
Emma Sherwood	121
Rachel Gilmour	122
Ricky Jones	122

Martin Smith	123
Lisa Goodrich	123
Oliver Newman	124
Andrew Morgan	124
Andrew Logan	125
Kayleigh Kirkman	126
Kylie Nancollas	126
Emily Pargeter	127
Christopher Atherton	127
Catriona Gilmour	127
Emma Houghton	128
Jenny Atkinson	128
Mark Stevenson	129
Sophie Milne	130
Lucy Lambert	130
Sarah Parkinson	131
Ceri Polglass	131
Chris Eves	132
Lydia Woodman	133
Gareth Freeman	134
Emma Howman	134
Callum Gibson	135
Rebecca Thirsk	135
Alex Clare	135
Thomas Beard	136
Holly Evans	136
Donna Kryger	137
Joshua Dean	138
Katie Garner	138
Hayley West	139
Christopher Moore	139
Steven Quayle	140
Sam Chapman	141
Jessica Hagerty	141
Lauren Truscott	142
Roy Doodson	142
Matthew Petch	142
Serge Beynon	143

Andrea Rugen	143
Amy Challenor	143
Stuart Jamieson	144
Christopher Popplestone	144
Suzanne Page	145
Emma Johnson	145
Alex Martin	146
Kim O'Grady	146
Katie White	147
Frances Buckley	147
Katy Wilson	148
Richard Cain	149
Kathryn James	150
Nathan Booth	150
Beth Anderson	151
Martin Williams	152
Nicole Tooze	152
Stephen Shields	153
Kevin Tierney	154
Rebecca Beech	155
Joseph Woodman	155
Jessica Woods	156
Philip Atkinson	157
Jesse Dean	158
David Bucknell	158
Naomi Hall	159
Carla Peters	159
Helen Wood	160
Deryn Blythe	160
David Wade	161
Sarah O'Connor	162
Gareth Evans	162
Philip Procter	163
Samantha Cain	163
Leon Hewitt	163
Steven Goodwin	164
Kim Donal	165
Michael Lawrence	166

Peter Blain 166
Sarah Brookes 167
Emma Davies 167
Kayley Hughes 168
Steven Smith 168
Katy Tomlin 169
Stacey Christie 169
Tom Steggel 170
Jamie Fleet 170
Neil Jacob 171
Helen Walker 171
Elizabeth Newton 172
Lauren Davies 172
Sarah Yould 173
Lois Norman 173
Peter Naylor 174
Victoria-Jade Tidbury 174
Davelee Brocklehurst 175
Helen Fuller 175
Annie Stewart 175
Jack Lightfoot 176
Eileen Greenwood 176
Emma Walker 177
Siobhan Eyes 177
Olive Hynes 178

Heath Comprehensive School
Sarah Hallam 179
Lee Hartigan 179
Mike Delaney 180
Sarah Perraton 180
Harry Mills 181
Thomas McNamara 181
Hayley Garnett 182
Gary Davies 182
Paul Gavin 183
Gary Inett 184
Charlotte Johnson 184

Nathan Davies	185
Adam Jones	186
Samantha Hawkins	186
Sarah-Jane Getty	187
Sophie Allan	187
Natalie Fletcher	188
Jessica Agnew	188
Leanne Wike	189
Scott Swales	189
Michaela Rowlinson	190
Danielle Duncalf	190
Alissa Tyrer	191
Lois Browne	191
Andrew Nelson	192
Beth Birmingham	192
Dawn Milliken	193
Michael Faragher	193
Laura Kinsley	194
Adam Glover	194
Michelle Dwerryhouse	195
Zoey Robb	196
Kevin Stoba	197
Andrew Wike	198
Rebecca Jayne Hough	198
Emma Callan	199
Jaclyn Thomas	199
Laura McGimpsey	200
Sadie Blythe	200
Heather Birmingham	201
Gemma Leach	202
Vicki Wood	202
Daniel Parkinson	203
Sarah Carter	203
Lisa Gavin	204
Laura Bate	204
Mathew Booth	205
Daniel Sankey	205
Laura Lacey	206

Tom Hulse	206
Wendy Osborne	207
Kayleigh McMillan	208
Joanne Illidge	208
Hayley Gavin	209
Siobhan Gibbons	209
Nicola Johnston	210
Roxanne Philip	210
Nicola Griffiths	211
Becky Barber	212
Sara Holt	212
Zoe Richards	213
Anthony Myers	213
Alex Parsons	214
Louise Berry	215
Rebecca Jones	215
Sarah Hoyland	216
Victoria Stanley	216
Jamie Caza	217
Stacey Johnson	217
Tom Morris	218
Kelly Gleave	218
Hayley Mountford	219
Lindsey Gittins	219
David Tomlinson	220
Stacey Malvern	221
Nicole Schofield	222
Thomas Smith	222
Ashley Ettrick	223
David Mayock	224
Philip Light	224

Knutsford High School

David Horsley	225
Sophie Norman	226
Charlotte Mann	227
Holly Poynton	228
Helen Roberts	229

Sarah Mason 229
Rebecca Weston 230
Alice Pemberton 231
Felicity Hutcheson 232
Kathryn Harrison 233

Longdendale High School
Andrew Davies 233
Ryan Moyles 234
Stephen Maher 234
Hannah Searle 235
Lee Robertson 236
Mark Foote 237
Adam Gee 238
Jodie Wilde 239
Niall Fawcett 239
Claire Aitken 240
Cathryn Kidd 240
Renée Fleming 241
Danielle Hinchliffe 241
Jennifer Bennett 242
David Batty 242
Jaime Elizabeth Briggs 243
Paul McClusky 243
Bill Kalaher 244
Heather Tolley 245
Rahaymin Chowdhury 246
Ben Hope 247
Heather Morgan 247
Sarah Bunyan 248
Francesca Davies 248
Stephanie Suthern 249
Rebecca Bolton 250
Emma Willingham 251
Lewis Bradley 251
Sasha Doherty 252
Melissa Barker 253
Amy Louise Noble 254

Rebecca Martens	254
Lee Allcock	255

Ryles Park County High School

Alice Hyde	256
Claire Gatley	258
Michael Clarke	258
Leanne Sarah Lee	259
Gemma McDonald	259
Luke Edwards	260
Lee Fitzgerald	260
Sophie Hodkinson	261
Allan Alili	261
Becky Trueman	262
Tara Bayley	262
Lee Dixon	263
Wendy Bowyer	263
Luke Hartley	264
Luke McDonald	264
Linda Phiri	265
Joy King	266
Liam Alcock	266
Simon Mayo	267
Tom Biggar	268
Adam Trelfa	268
Sarah Lomas	269
Gareth Maartens	269
Christopher Adams	270

Sir Thomas Boteler High School

Callum Smythe	270
Scott Fisher	271
Bruce McKinnon	271
Reece Hampton	272
Fatima Rahman	272
Lauren Himme	272
Brian Dickeson	273
Scott Thomas Whitfield	273

Toby Roy Barnett 273
Ben Kenyon 274
Louise Dack 274
Siobhan Davies 274
Sam Dean 275
James Boucher 275
Ryan Edwardson 276

Wilmslow County High School
Owen Davies 276
Gemma Connell 277
Nick Bazley 278
Alison Jones 280
Sara O'Grady 280
Scott Taylor 281
Josie Haslam 282
Grace Emily Thorneycroft 282
Emma Kerr 283
Jake Gill 284
Alex Doherty 285
Paul Richardson 286
Thomas Larkman 286
Rachel Moss 287
James Newton 288
Kathryn Evans 289
Claire Chadwick 290
Abby Newell 291
Hayley Williams 292
John Drinkwater 293

The Poems

ARE YOU AFRAID OF THE DARK?

As I walk down the street
There's nothing to hear.
This is the feeling
That fills me with fear.

As I walk round the corner
I'm full of fear.
I'm looking at a wall
Wondering what will I hear.

As I walk up the road
I feel a cool breeze.
I'm now so terrified
Looking at the dark scary trees.

As I walk up my garden path
All the lights are out.
I'm now so terrified
Help I would like to shout.

As I open my door
There's no noise to be heard.
Now though I know
There's no need to be scared.

I walk upstairs where my daughter's asleep
I open the door and just catch a peep
I walk in her room and then to her bed
There is my daughter lying there dead!

Jacob Howden (12)
Bankfield High School

HOW TIME FLIES THROUGH A CHILD'S EYES!

In the morning I began to fret,
To wake up from my dreaming bed.
To go to a place unknown to me,
To wear a tie and shirt with sleeves.

With pens to write and text to read,
The alphabet will have a need.
To learn to read, write and sing,
But not to talk, fight and steal.

But in the playground I will meet,
Friends that grow on me.
To play a lot and
Come to my house for tea.

The big boys would pick on me,
Beat and punch and make me bleed.
I would then sit in a corner,
Cry and cry for now I wonder,
What school would be like without the blunder.

Aeden McGuffie (13)
Bankfield High School

A DAY IN THE LIFE

One day on the telephone,
The dog choking on a bone,
My eyes were close to tears,
I had so many fears.

He fell to the floor,
As I opened the door,
A man shot a bird, as I occurred.

He sat there talking,
In the morning,
As I heard a squeal,
I fell over a wheel.

Then at night, I had a fight,
In the gloom,
Was a moon.

Sean Andrews (12)
Bankfield High School

THE CAT

One day when I was alone in the woods
Something caught my eye.
A small black object sitting in the buds,
Gingerly watching by.

As I grew closer to the buds,
The animal became scarce
A loud rustling noise shook the woods
And the animal stood there.

I realised now it was a cat
As it prowled around my feet.
Not one which snuggles up in a mat
But who hunts the woods for meat.

I don't think it has been or seen inside a house,
But as I looked back for the cat
It scurried after a mouse.

Ben Hickton (12)
Bankfield High School

UNTITLED

Tell us Mum again
When you went on a plane
Was it good or was it fun?
Did you lay in the sun?
Did you arrive at day or night?
Did you ever get into a fight?

Okay kids gather round
I'll tell you about when I
Landed on the ground
It was great and it was cool
And I laid in the pool.

I went out at night
But then I saw a fight
I tried to stop it but I was too late
Somebody already fell to their fate.

Then I saw a mouse on the floor
And it looked very small
I chased it round and round
Until I collapsed on the ground
I was very dizzy, I could not see
Someone was looking over me.

She picked me up
And took me to her home
And that is where
I had my own telephone.

So did you enjoy it?
I enjoyed it a bit
Okay then
Now go on and play in your pen.

Robin Farrington (13)
Bankfield High School

CLIMBING

I'm
Climbing up,
Up ever so high,
Higher than the clouds,
When I reach the sky.
I will prove I am right,
By showing everyone
That I can, I can,
I can reach the sky.
I will be the best,
I will rule,
I will be totally cool.
I can't wait to see their faces,
They will be so happy,
I can't wait to see their faces
The world will be so *joyful.*

Kimberley Littler (12)
Bankfield High School

FLASH LIKE FIRE

I flash like fire,
I glow like the moon,
I twinkle like the stars from above,
I fly like an eagle and sting like a bee,
I fall like the rain.

I bring peace and tranquillity,
I am a teddy bear, all sweet and innocent,
I am the green grass swaying in the calm
Summer's breeze.

Sophie Bowman (12)
Bankfield High School

BET YOU'RE SCARED

My mum's scared,
My dad's scared,
Everyone I know is scared.
Those hairy legs, those tiny eyes
And that tickly feeling
When they crawl on you
Sends shivers down your spine
But really, they are just little black dots,
Crawling all over your socks
You know what I mean because
You're probably scared of
Spiders too!

Martin Jackson (11)
Bankfield High School

SPACE

In space
there are bright, bright stars
most of them come from Mars.
If one star goes out of control
then the solar system
will become a black hole.
The moon and the sun are the shape of
a cheeseburger bun.
In space there are lots of planets
I like Jupiter, Saturn and Pluto too.
Do you like them?
Because I do.

Tom Beattie (11)
Bankfield High School

MARS

Whizzing and whirling,
Up, up and away.
Spinning and twirling,
Far from Earth.
Turning and swirling,
We've landed, what next?
Here we are walking on Mars!
No, look an ugly pink spotted monster!
Hoping and praying it won't eat us alive.
Sneakily pulling our ray guns ready to kill,
Getting ready to zap it,
Bang, it's gone, we're walking around
Aargh, it's got me!
It's dragging me back to its hole!
There, there are some of its brothers.
What are they going to do?
Oh no, there's more, a green one
Poof, it's killed them!
It's running and gasping with me!
I'm back, I'm alive here at my rocket
Oh joy! Oh hope!
I'm waving goodbye.
Whizzing and whirling
Going down, down and away.

Rebecca Naylor (11)
Bankfield High School

JOBS

When I'm older the jobs I don't want are
A writer?
I don't want blocks everywhere!
A postman?
I don't want to get up early!
A teacher?
I still want my voice at the end of the day!
A secretary?
Too much hard thinking!
An artist?
Too messy and difficult!
An air hostess?
The food's horrible and you get too dizzy!
A policewoman?
Too dangerous!
A lawyer?
You have to be too narky!

Natalie Russell (11)
Bankfield High School

THE DAY IN THE LIFE OF FRANCIAS FOX

As I walked through the forest one day,
Suddenly, just then,
Out from a brush quite far away,
Poked a black thing with a human on the end.

I started running through the forest
All of a sudden,
Something he had molested,
Was now that man's pudding.

I went back to my burrow,
To get away and out of this nightmare in hell,
To find that my wife had gone,
With the children as well.

Then I started to think and think,
Then suddenly I thought,
That thing he'd shot in the wood,
Could have been my wife he'd caught.

Kayleigh Snelson (13)
Bankfield High School

UNTITLED

Nothing, no life, no world, no me or you.
Then it became clear with an ear splitting bang.
The large round planets turning, twisting in the atmosphere,
There was one planet in a perfect position, perfect for us. Earth.
If you looked closely you could see the blue sky
Wrapping itself around the sphere.
Never-ending still water glistening in the sunlight.
Enormous snow-capped mountains, their peaks above the clouds.
Dipping valleys leading to the green, bushy pine forests.
Leaves on the trees blowing gently in the breeze.
The delicate flowers turning to obey the rays of sunlight.
Birds in flight peacefully drifting through the air,
Bees circling around the flowers,
Children playing in the park, cheekily annoying their parents.
Life on Earth seems a nice place to be.
It is there for you and me.

Julia Giblin (11)
Bankfield High School

SURVIVAL

As you lived your life in fear,
that dreadful siren screamed again.
People rushed into shelters and subways,
to be safe from death.
As you listened . . . listened . . .
you heard a buzz, then a wail,
a long deafening which got louder and louder until
there was a bang, a thud, and a terrible sense from outside.
The first glimpse of what will happen during the night.
As you try to rest you find yourself having bad dreams about how
you will survive. A tear rolls down your cheek.
Louder and louder night gets until early morning,
when the final bomb has been dropped and the raid is over.
People walked out of their shelters and were struck with terror,
homes had been destroyed,
people had been killed,
memories lost, and families torn apart by a void.
People had to do the best they could today,
to survive another raid tonight.

Craig Leech (11)
Bankfield High School

FRIENDSHIP!

Friendship is all a person needs,
It's one of God's golden deeds.
Today and forever they will always care,
As long as you are always there.

Friends are there when you are sad,
They will help you when times are bad.
When you feel down and glum,
They make you laugh and have lots of fun.

You can make friends with people you don't know,
Friends you make may come and go,
The ones that stay forever there,
Are friends who really, really care.

Amy Burns (12)
Bankfield High School

DIFFERENT SHOPS

Our shops are full of sweets,
Toys and TV magazines.

I think the lottery is even worse,
I really think it is a curse.

You never win and you get upset,
Then you think buying it was a regret.

Sweets! Rotten teeth, aching tooth,
Then you want to go to McDonald's food booth.

The papers are okay to read,
Usually inside the paper you get a free packet of seeds.

Fizzy pop, ice-cold drinks,
And computers that think.

Toys, CDs, videos and DVDs

We're all not rich,
We're all not made of money,
Don't waste it on junk,
It's not funny.

Amy Connor (11)
Bankfield High School

THE JOURNEY

Moving softly at a very slow pace,
The craft journeys on across the void of space.
Whatever dangers may arise,
The craft is hidden by its mere size.

The craft drifts along at its steady speed,
In space it is merely a tiny seed.
It journeys on and on and on,
Until sight of it is almost gone.

Through solar systems it will go,
Sometimes fast and sometimes slow.

Through the cosmos it will twist and bend,
But to the craft this journey will . . . never end.

Paul Kitching (11)
Bankfield High School

HALLOWE'EN

Hallowe'en is so much fun,
we knock on the doors
and then we run.
Sometimes we stay,
get sweets and money
or some apples dipped in honey.
We carry our pumpkin,
we wear our masks,
when we walk along, the people gasp.
We then go home and up to bed
and hope we don't see the man with no head.

Mark Duckett (12)
Bankfield High School

WINSTON AND I

Winston and I
What a funny name you say!

Winston don't dangle
You'll get yourself
In a tangle.
You know you don't oughta
Oh dear
Now you've fell
In the water.

You should have more sense
But I know you're a bit dense.

Then you're only a baby,
A pretty parrot too
Pretty parrot, pretty parrot
I love you.

Lauren Gee (12)
Bankfield High School

DOVES

Birds are a wonderful creature of the world.
I think that the best one of all is
The whitest dove, that sings so sweet.

The dove is so brilliant at flying through the air,
It has no worries and no enemies.

Just sitting there is a beautiful sight,
Its smooth feathers shine so bright, in the sunlight.

Jessica Mercer (11)
Bankfield High School

I FLASH LIKE FIRE!

I flash like fire
In the skies above
And the rain comes down
Like a falling dove.

I am as strong as a lion
But as light as a feather
I float to the ground
For eternity, forever.

I hear the raindrops
Bouncing off the ground,
I hear everything
I don't miss a sound.

I see the mist
It covers the sky,
I wait for the thunder
A blink of the eye.

The moon shines brightly
All around,
The stars are glistening
There isn't a sound.

Louise McNabb (12)
Bankfield High School

THE VAMPIRE

In one mysterious night
The vampire will awaken
With his fangs baring he will bite
And someone's life will be taken

As the full moon shines
The outline of a bat can be seen
If you want to get rid of him
You will have to call a slayer team.

Johnnie Padilla (13)
Bankfield High School

IN THE NIGHT

I flash like fire
In the night, in the night
Like a roaring star
In the night, in the night
I'm as strong as the wind
In the night, in the night
To fly so very far
In the night, in the night.

Now I can't flash like fire
In the night, in the night
Not like a roaring star
In the night, in the night
I'm not as strong as the wind
In the night, in the night
Can't fly so very far
In the night, in the night.

The sun is rising
So send me your love
I'm weakening, I'm weakening
So send me your love!

Anna Kilgariff (13)
Bankfield High School

WHY CAN'T GIRLS BE BOYS AND BOYS BE GIRLS?

Why doesn't Daddy do the washing up
or hoover up the hall?
Why doesn't Mummy mend the car
or go and play football?
Why doesn't Daddy sew my clothes
or change the baby's bed?
Why doesn't Mummy stay out late
drinking with her friends instead?

Why did Daddy buy my brother
guns and football boots
Action Man and cars and trains
and dress him up in blue?
Why does Mummy buy my sister
soft pink clothes to wear
Dolls that cry and wet their prams
and lifelike growing hair?

Why do boys get dirty
when girls are so pristine?
Why do boys help Dad outside
when girls help Mum to clean?
Why are boys told that it's right
to fight and wrong to cry?
Why are girls taught to say 'Yes'
and never question why?

Why can boys be nasty when girls have to be nice?

Why are boys like slugs and snails and girls like sugar and spice?

Johnathan Harrison (12)
Bankfield High School

FLASH LIKE FIRE

I flash like fire
In the dawning of the day,
I glow in the dark
With a fire in my heart.

In the dusk of the day I am fading away
With one last flash I fade from today,
Until tomorrow I will come again.

In the dusk of the day I am fading away
And then,
Flash! And crash!

I go till I fade away to cease to be until I am nothing
But a twinkle in the corner of your eye.

Ashley Hulse (12)
Bankfield High School

THE SUN

He's blazing down on half the world,
Looking at what he can see.
With a big cheesy grin, he pulls down his shades,
And gives a little wink.
While he watches the children sing and dance,
One sneaks a lolly ice.
The clouds try to hide him
But that doesn't work.
He bursts out with an awful tear
A few hours more and he won't be there,
The few hours passed, he was no longer there,
Everyone was sleeping so that half the world was a blur.

Kerry-Ann Baynton (12)
Bankfield High School

I FLASH LIKE FIRE

I flash like fire
Filled with desire,
I shine like the sun
On everyone,
I glow like the moon
Lighting the lake.

I howl like the wind
Blowing the trees,
I flash like lightning
And light the world,
I fall like snow
On ice-capped mountains.

Yvonne Morris (12)
Bankfield High School

I FLASH LIKE FIRE

I flash like fire
I'm the morning star,
I am the thunder
Heard from afar.

I am a rainbow
Arched above,
I glow like a star
I fly like a dove.

I am a teardrop
Falling to the ground,
I am a shark
I don't make a sound.

Alison Lea (12)
Bankfield High School

I FLASH LIKE FIRE

I flash like fire,
I gleam like a block of gold,
I shine like the sun,
And I'm extremely bold.

I flash like fire,
I clash like a rock,
I'm as bright as a star,
But take my time like a clock.

I flash like fire in the midnight sky, as the moon
Lights up every corner in the universe.
The sun takes over the darkness
Until it is reversed.

Andrew Mines (12)
Bankfield High School

I FLASH LIKE FIRE

I flash like fire,
The eternal light,
When the air is cold,
And in the night,
I lead the way,
Like a shining star,
So high, high, high in the sky.

I flow like water,
And extinguish the flame,
Through my fight to the sea,
I'll once again be free,
I flash like fire!

Adam Jackson (13)
Bankfield High School

AS I DRIFT AWAY

I flash like fire
In the blazing sun,
I glow like a star
Upon everyone.

I roar like thunder
I shine like the sun,
I'm as clear as the sky
In the day to come.

I howl like the wind
On a dull, gloomy day,
I hear the rustle of the leaves
As they get blown away.

I hear the patter of the rain
Fall onto the ground,
I hear the hailstone lashing down
I hear every sound.

I see the fog forming
As cloudy as ever,
I can't see far
It goes on forever.

I sway like the trees
On a windy autumn day,
I'm as grey as the skies
As I drift away . . .

Lucy Downham (12)
Bankfield High School

I FLASH LIKE FIRE

I flash like fire
I glisten like a star,
I glow like a flame
I shine like the sun,
I flash like lightning
I clash like thunder
As the moon glows in the evening sky.

I'm the colour of the sky
As pure as the clouds,
I'm as still as a river
As calm as the breeze on a summer's day.

I'm as cold as snow and
As warm as a fire
I'm the sparkle that's in everyone's eye.

Karen Shaw (12)
Bankfield High School

THROUGH A HAMSTER'S EYES

As I wandered out of my open cage,
I jumped onto the floor,
When I just missed the door.
I was in the dining room under the table,
When I just missed being stood on.
I escaped out of the way of the kicking feet,
Into the living room.
When my journey had to come to an end,
I could see the telly
Yes! Pet Rescue was on . . .

Hayden Lee (12)
Bankfield High School

UPON EVERYONE

I flash like fire
I glow like the sun,
I shine like a star
Upon everyone.

I crash like lightning
I flash like thunder,
Bringing you love,
Bringing you hope.

I am the colour of a rainbow
I am as strong as the sea.
I shine like a star,
Upon everyone.

I flow like a river
I soar through the sky,
A shooting star
Bringing you love,
Bringing you hope.

Beth Hughes (13)
Bankfield High School

FLASH LIKE FIRE

I flash like fire
Like a gleaming wire
Shining like the sun
I sparkle like a rich blue gem
I then flash like lightning again and again
I am the river clashing over the rocks
The colourful feathers upon the peacock.

I gurgle like a bubbling spring
Like a bluebird in summer I sing
I'm like the cattle running over the hills
I'm the colours on the puffin's bill
I fly with the bees
And I clash with the seas
I float through the forest as the gentle breeze.

Stephanie Chester (12)
Bankfield High School

FLASH LIKE FIRE

I flash like fire
I gleam like the stars
The night is coming
And I will soon.
But don't be afraid
Now the darkness has come
For the moon will protect us
Till we next see the sun.

I flash like fire
I flow like the sea
I shine like the sun
Come shine with me.

I flash like fire in the dark of the night
A glance of my face is an awesome sight
I blast fire from my mouth
And smoke from my nose.
Ask all the villagers for they know
Because I am the dragon . . .

Thomas McGauley (12)
Bankfield High School

ANOTHER DAY OF SPORT

Another day of sport,
My kit, my mum hasn't bought,
A football match tomorrow,
I suppose I'll have to borrow,
But today I'm playing football
And I haven't brought my boots,
I'll just have to ask my mum,
So I can have some fun.
I wish I had the ability
So I could have the agility.

Another day of sport,
A kit my mum has bought,
Now I can play sport,
We draw nought-nought.
Rugby match next week,
Got detention for giving cheek,
So I cannot play,
With a look of dismay.

William Buckley (11)
Bankfield High School

HAUNTED HOUSE

A haunted house, he sits alone,
Speaks to no one for he has no phone,
The day breaks, he tries to hide,
His vines cover him far and wide.

Soon night falls,
And his wild cats call,
His bats come out,
And his goblins shout.

He hears the shot of a murderless gun,
Perhaps it's time to demolish the sun,
Child's play he likes no more,
Especially when they come knocking on his door.

He's beginning to get warm,
And his vines creep up,
The sun has arrived.

Alicia Ann Dunning (11)
Bankfield High School

CASTLE IN THE SKY

As I sit there, in my mind's eye
I see a magical castle in the sky.
It has several boats,
Sailing in its several moats.

Vast cannons firing cannon balls,
To show that it is twelve o'clock.
But inside, there are drapes coating the halls,
And ancient paintings showing relatives,
Even a man from Scotland called Jock.

But oh so strange, there are no people,
No king or queen
No squire or servant
Neither a vicar in steeple.

Oh this was only a dream,
A nice dream
Not a nasty nightmare,
That would make a young child scream.

What a magical dream!

Neil Devany (11)
Bankfield High School

AUTUMN

It's time for autumn, my worst season of the year.
5, 4, 3, 2, 1, I'm off, swirling, twirling like a rollercoaster
Through the trees, over rooftops but never a word my uncle said.
Here's the road I dread to drive, but I suppose I have to go
I'm afraid the wind will die down on me
Oh no
       D
             O
                   W
                        N
                             I go
Landing on the damp road and down the drain
Into the slimy sewers I'm afraid I have to go now
My uncle's just gone past me.

Adele Mew (11)
Bankfield High School

FLASH LIKE FIRE

I flash like fire,
I shine like the sun.
I'm independent like
When a young parts
With its parent.
I'd like to be a hypnotist
To get the things I'd like,
I'd like to be an animal
Because I'd be free of
Stress and tension.
This is my poem
Of how I am and
What I feel.

David Tickle (12)
Bankfield High School

EVERTON

All the teams in The Premiership
I pick one 'Everton'
Everton are the best
Better than the rest
Everton score goals
They play for their souls
Fans run around like mad
But they're not that bad
Campbell, Fergie are my players
Man U are the slayers
Even though Leicester are at the top
Everton will not stop
I'll support Everton all the way
Till that day!

Luke Jackson (11)
Bankfield High School

MATCH OF THE DAY

Match Of The Day is great,
With Gary Lineker's big ears,
And Mark Lawrenson's bushy moustache,
And Trevor Brooking's cockney accent,
They all present the best football highlights,
Tony Adams trying, David Ginola diving,
Michael Owen scoring even though the match was boring,
Duncan Ferguson moving, proving how good he is,
Leeds United sponsored by Nike,
Before the match the kit is lovely and white,
Man United buying, everyone trying,
Then Gary Lineker flying with those Dumbo ears.

Michael Wilson (11)
Bankfield High School

PEACE

People want peace, not war,
   Everyone wants peace, please follow the law,
Animals, people, children too,
   Could be safe if you were to do,
Everything that is right.

In this world, on this night,
   Never have war, please don't fight.

Towns, people need you, do what is right,
   Have you ever thought of children in their bed,
Everyone wondering whether they will be dead?

Would our world ever be the same,
   Or will it go down in shame?
Right now in the world nothing's going on,
   Love and happiness have not gone.
Dreams and hopes will carry on.

So can you see how good it will be with
Peace in the world!

Danielle Buckley (11)
Bankfield High School

PUSSY, PUSSY

Sleeping proudly on a chair
When you hear a quiet purr.
As she wakes up, stretch
She walks as proud as a queen.

As she walks and stops to get fed
She will not be led.
As she goes out to play
She walks past an unkindly stray.

As she has finished scrapping
With the stray she carries on her way.
As she keeps on walking
She meets her sister, they play all day.

As they lay their heads to sleep,
And they fall to bed counting sheep.

Daniel Whitfield (12)
Bankfield High School

LEAVES

Back and forth, back and forth,
Blown from every leafless tree,
How beautiful my life could be,
Sitting here without any rhythm,
Back and forth this toothless, withered leaf,
Back and forth, back and forth,
I always end up in the sky,
Sometimes it makes me crazy, well my mind's eye,
Maybe I'll have a bee,
Or maybe one will land on me,
Back and forth, back and forth,
Oh me, oh my,
How I wish I could fly,
When I want to get away,
I just spread out and I don't stay,
It's not here I want to be so
The wind carries me far and free.
Back and forth,
Back and forth,
Back and forth, back and forth!

Joe Fitzsimon (11)
Bankfield High School

A BURGLARY AT THE PALACE

When the Queen returned to her golden throne
She looked forward to sitting down
She reached across to her little table
And found there was no crown

She shouted into Prince Peter
And quickly he ran in
'My dear Peter, my crown has gone'
'My dear Queen, I'll check the bin'

Prince Peter was in such a flap
He ran into the room that's been painted
He came out and searched high and low
But when he returned she had fainted

'Oh no, my beloved Queen
Do you feel alright?'
'Get away you stupid man
You gave me such a fright'

'Look my Queen there goes the thief'
'What that black and white bird?
Don't you be so silly,
Don't you be so absurd

Now I've got it in my sight
Quick get up off your trifle'
'Yes, Your Majesty, whatever you say
Now shoot it with that rifle.'

Emma Prendergast (11)
Bankfield High School

WALKABOUT

As I am dying I think of my family and remember
Mother's cooking that I could die for,
My father and his fascinating stories,
My grandmother's glowing smile.

The things I never saw and the things I did see.
Darkness of the sky at night,
Sun at dawn,
The desert in the moonlight.

I have also seen and heard the sound of nature,
The howling wind,
The mournful cries of the dingo,
The minute rattle of the rattlesnake.

My emotions are different every hour of every day,
Disappointment that I will never complete my journey,
Anger, not knowing what I have done wrong,
Loneliness knowing I am all alone.

Why am I dying?
When am I going to die?
Where will I die?
These I do not know.

Andrew Robinson (13)
Bankfield High School

I LOOK OUT OVER THE PLAIN

I look out over the plain
Wonder when I will die
Saw the look the lubra gave me
Tomorrow?
Today?
Next week?

I look out over the plain
Wonder whether family will miss me
Broken-hearted?
I never finished my walkabout.

I look out over the plain
I will miss the things I have known
I will miss the golden sand
Between my toes
Taste of sparkling water in my mouth
Smell of the wallaby cooking over the hot fire.

I look out over the plain
Would I have been married?
Beautiful Billadad, the girl of my dreams!
Children to pass on the power of the tribe?
Gaze into someone's eyes.

I look out over the plain,
I wonder about the feelings I have inside me.

Sadness,
Regret,
Failure,
Anger
All these but no one to talk to
Will just have to wait for my death
Waiting
Looking out over the plain.

Alison Leadbetter (13)
Bankfield High School

ELEPHANTS

They're big and heavy
they stomp around all day,
and they flap their thin ears to keep the flies away.

They have a bath each day
to keep nice and cool,
they will lie for a rest in the shade
or splash in the pool.

They all have big feet, four of them,
and a long trunk.

They like rolling in the mud
and then being cleaned in the pool.

Have you guessed it yet,
it's also very strong,
and has a body coloured grey,
it's an elephant!

Michelle Richards (11)
Bankfield High School

LONELINESS

Cold, calming wind brushes
Carelessly past my face.
I gaze beyond the distance
Rippling Billabong,
Gum tree adorned with multicoloured budgerigars.
Lone wombat
Scuttling to night's shelter
All dwarfed by the domination of the setting sun sundering the day.

Aware of the lubra and little one's reliance on me
I must lead them to the valley,
Before the stalker claims my spirit,
Or one life
Will lead to three claimed.

Sadness,
Anger,
Failure,
Regret,
Alone!
Afraid!
The spirit of death
Contemplates my time.
Why?
Why?
Have I offended someone?
Hurt somebody?
Done something wrong?
Why?

Never again will I taste a warawora,
Sweet as a red berry in the
Month of blooming petals,
Smell the fresh morning dew.

Never again will I see my mother always full of joy,
My brave father,
My valiant tribe,
The beauty of a golden sunrise,
A newborn wombat,
A gum tree in full bloom.

A triumphant ceremony for my return,
Is only a dream.
But I won't sleep,
I must not sleep,
I wait,
Wait.

Jenny McGauley (13)
Bankfield High School

THE SNOWMAN

December's the time when snowmen are made.
The ground is white and fluffy.
Hats, scarves and gloves are worn to keep the children happy.
When Christmas morning comes
the children are all excited, they run down the stairs,
sit on the chairs and wait for their parents to come.

So they get dressed, have breakfast and set off to build a snowman.
They start off by making the head, starting small, getting tall.
To make the body they roll the snow,
their gloves are wet, they build it big and they've finished it.
The children add a hat, and scarf, they put a carrot for the nose,
coal for the eyes and coal for the mouth.
They put coal on the body for the buttons
and the children have made the perfect snowman.

Dawn Mason (11)
Bankfield High School

WHY?

When will I enter the valley of death?
Why have I failed?
Why?
Why?
Oh why am I going to the valley of death?

I will miss the tribe
The party when I return
I will never see my family again
What about the children?
I've got to get them to the springs
Will I last that long?
Oh how quickly do I need to get them to the spring?

I won't have children
I won't know what it's like to be a man
I won't have a wife
Oh why me?
Why?
Why?

Was it medicine man who put the shadow of death over me?
The shadow of death!
The shadow of death!
Why is the shadow of death hanging over me?

Never again will I smell the sweet smell of a cooking wallaby
Never again will I taste the juicy meat of a wallaby
Never again will I hear the melodious sound of a pardalote
Never again will I touch a rough yucca root
Never again will I see the exquisite sunset
Why is it me entering the valley of death?
Why?
Why?
Why?

Iain McConnell (13)
Bankfield High School

FLASH LIKE FIRE

I flash like fire,
From the ripples in the water,
I flash as if I was fire,
Roaring through the day,
As the sun shines,
I gleam,
As the moon shines,
I glisten,
When the sky is dull,
I am colourless,
Lifeless,
In a world of my own,
I roar through the day,
With intense heat,
I am as big as a skyscraper,
But also a seed.

Danny Roberts (12)
Bankfield High School

DEATH!

I look out upon the plain
Faced with death itself
Death!
When I am gone
Goodbye my tribe
I can't survive
I can't survive

Must get them to the valley
Or death's around the boulder
Death!
When I am gone
The children die
They can't survive
They can't survive

I am their aid
Their life support
If I die
They die too
Death!
When I am gone
The children die
They can't survive
They can't survive

Where is my mother?
Need her here
Miss her gleaming smile
Death!
When I am gone
Goodbye my tribe
I can't survive
I can't survive

My 'future wife' will be so sad
My life was such a waste
Death!
When I am gone
Goodbye my tribe
I can't survive
I can't survive

Death!

Keith Schofield (13)
Bankfield High School

HALLOWE'EN

It is Hallowe'en time
Where the beasties awake
Everybody goes around
Chorusing trick or treats.

When the end is nigh they
Go home to eat their sweets.

Ghosts, ghouls they all come
Out on a night like no other
(It's just the right time to
Scare your little sister or brother).

The sweets are ready
We are all dressed up
We are ready to go
Bags at the hand we are
Ready for a night of spooks and scares.

Rebecca O'Connor (11)
Bankfield High School

WAITING

I am standing, standing alone
Standing in ebony and moonlight
Waiting
Waiting for what was yet to come
Death
Awaiting me in darkness and loneliness
How am I to die?
Will it come quickly or slowly?
How will it feel?
Painful or peaceful?

What will I miss when I am gone?
Being near to my family and friends
Enjoying the rest of my tribe perform their songs and dances
Seeing my parents' faces when I arrive back
After completing my walkabout
My sister enjoying the special celebration food

The things I will never have
A wife
Children of my own
Seeing my own son complete his walkabout
A future
A life
All these things I will not live to see

I am standing, standing alone
Standing in ebony and moonlight
Waiting
Waiting for what was yet to come
Death
Waiting.

Sarah Lister (13)
Bankfield High School

WALKABOUT

Wondering whether this is the last time,
The last time I hear the singing lark,
Watching the sunset on the horizon,
The rattle of the king serpent.

Thinking of those memories
Mum!
Dad!
Brother!
Sister!
Friends!
This is the last time.

No future ahead - wife, children, happiness,
Who knows?
Only time will tell,
But I do know the spirit of death will rest upon me.

I'll miss having Father boasting about the battles he has
Fought and won,
Mother cooking,
Brother, sister fighting,
Friends laughing, joking.

The last time,
I will face my fear,
The spirit of death will rest,
It's my turn . . .
My turn . . .
My turn . . .

Stephen Bounds (13)
Bankfield High School

THE BUSH BOY'S THOUGHTS

Silence of the night
Except from the singing lark's songs
Animals coming to feed
I stare lonely.

Afraid.

The whisper of the wind
Like my grandmother's voice
Soft
I see her face.

Afraid.

What have I done wrong?
I do not know
Lubra saw death in me
Will I die?

Will I dance again?
Father, Mother
Funny games we play at night
Like the dingo.

Afraid.

What will I miss?
Thoughts running through my mind
My brother giving me advice
Like the warning of the rattlesnake.

I thought I could be a leader
Not any more
In a way I am now
Leading these children.

I will die strong like a hurricane not weak like a whimpering dingo
The spirit of death won't take three
I need to take them where they can survive
Where there is water and food.

Phil Woodward (13)
Bankfield High School

AUTUMN DAYS

The cold wind blows,
    Got icy toes,
I want to go to bed
    Crunchy leaves and bare trees
And hot and crispy bacon.
    I love the sausage and the egg
for my warm cooked breakfast
    Sizzle, sizzle, sizzle, fry, sizzle, sizzle, fry.

The cold wind blows,
    Got icy toes,
I want to go to bed,
    Warm, white milk before I go
To warm my aching throat.

The cool wind blows,
    No icy toes,
The autumn and winter have gone
    I miss the snow but the rain
It is always the same

I wish it was the summer!

Carolyn Henry (11)
Bankfield High School

THE BUSH BOY'S LOOKOUT

Quietness is all around
Seems like death has come
How long?
Maybe I will go tonight
It may take a few days

Never have the chance to grow up strong
Have a wife
My own child

Never be able to play with friends
Watch the sun setting in the clear blue sky

Never see Mum
Or Dad
Never to see Grandma
Or taste her wonderful meals

I must hurry to get the white children to safety
If I shall die
They too would
Die!
Die!
Die!

Claire Swift (14)
Bankfield High School

THE BUSH BOY AWAITS

Here I am,
Without even a whisper of when death will come,
To disown me from the world,
Sad,
Lonely.

Wondering if I will ever see my friends again,
Inside I am angry,
Angry towards the one thing I can't avoid.
Death.

The word cuts through me like a sharp knife,
Not knowing when it will come to haunt me is even worse,
Will I ever see my family again?
Those who I will miss the most.

What will happen to the children?
They trust in me,
The Lubra, she has seen death in me,
I must accept that soon it will be here.

Without me death will win the fight,
Taking the children too,
Claiming two more.

But I'm still here waiting,
Beneath the diminishing sunset,
Patiently to see death's creeping approach,
Will it take me far, far away,
Far, far, far.

Claire Campbell (13)
Bankfield High School

FINAL THOUGHTS

Stand, in the shadow of death,
Not knowing what will happen next.

Come so far,
Done so well,
Near to completion,
My hope has gone,
My success diminished into pieces.

What have I done?
What went wrong?
Why was there death in the lubra's eye?
Why?

My life is the illusion of death,
Only faint and hopeful memories,
My tribe,
How I will miss them,
Their intricate dance,
Happy times we shared.
But,
Gone,
Never to see them again!

I will never see my parents,
My mother's glowing smile,
Taste the sweetness of the wallaby,
Nor hear the singing finches' cry

But I can't go yet,
They need my help,
I must take them,
I shall lead their way!

Lisa Vickerstaffe (14)
Bankfield High School

FINAL MOMENTS

Death's limp shadow dominates my life,
Darkening remaining days on Earth.
Hope of survival? Gone,
Hope of seeing my loving family slowly fading.

Will never forget memories we shared,
Unforgettable moments,
Death has come to take me away,
Can't escape its grasp.

What have I done wrong?

Angered someone?
Somewhere?
Somehow?
Angry at myself,
Hate the sense of not knowing.

Soon I shall die,
Where?
When?
How?

Lubra saw death in me,
Saw it in the depths of my eyes.

Death!
Soon I shall die.
Death!
Shadow that keeps out all life.

D
    E
        A
          T
            H

Jennifer Middleton (13)
Bankfield High School

SNOWFLAKES

Snowflakes drop
On a winter's day.
Snowflakes don't
Drop in the
Middle of May.
Snowflakes melt
In the summer's breeze.
Snowflakes drop
From winter trees.
Snowflakes dry up
When summer comes.
They come again
With carol songs.
Snowflakes are
Like a million crystals
Falling from the
Clouds then shot
By pistols.

Kieran McCarthy (11)
Bankfield High School

SCHOOL

School is to help you
Whether you like it or not
Go every day and learn a lot
Do English, maths, science and others,
And if you get stuck with your homework
Get help off your mothers and if it gets harder
And makes you feel bad all you do is
Ask your dad!

Lisa Anne Gatcliffe (11)
Bankfield High School

DAYDREAM WORLD

Sitting here
Watching telly
With a beer and some jelly
Suddenly I was in the picture
Running from Alfie Flitcher
Wandering around a haunted house
Scrambling from a 10ft mouse
He was big, he was hairy
But most of all he was *scary*
Trying to run but my feet won't move
They're stuck in concrete shoes
Where was I, how did I get here
And where's my beer?
Now I'm stuck in this flipping telly
Running from mice and villains, please
Somebody
Switch off the telly, after all it was a
Daydream.

Nathan Murphy (11)
Bankfield High School

STORM

Rain pounds on the windows like a hundred angry fists;
Lightning strikes like a light bulb smashing.
Thunder comes like a drum-playing band;
Black clouds come like growling bears.
Roads slippy like an ice rink;
Trees shaking like terrified people.
Wind howling like a witch's stew;
Sea is rough like a giant is swimming there.

Anna Marie Bredin (12)
Bankfield High School

MY PET DOG

My pet dog is small and soft
He plays with my socks.
He runs around like a Formula One racing car
Looks around like a spy in a tree
And spins around like a spinning top
And rolls around like a log rolling down a hill
Every day he chases after the milkman until 11.00
Then he sits down and barks at the postman
Woof
Woof
Woof
The postman runs
Clash, clash, clash
Goes the postman into the dustbin
It's the same every day.

David Woolfall (11)
Bankfield High School

ONE LITTLE MOUSE

One little mouse,
Lived in a house,
Eating a wonderful nut.
He was sad and lived all alone,
But one day he got a ring on his phone,
It was his friend who lived in a hut.
His friend came over for just one day,
But soon his friend had to go away,
The little mouse was really sad,
When his friend went away he felt really bad.

Gary Stevenson (11)
Bankfield High School

A CAT'S LIFE

I'd love to be a cat,
And lie by the fire on the mat.
I'd love to curl up in a ball,
Under the stairs in the hall.
I'd hang around by the trees,
Chasing all the busy bees.
I'd come back late, all alone
To be safe with my family at home.
I'd not have to tell where I've been,
Then come in and have a clean.
I'd have a drink and something to eat,
Then I'd have a lovely treat.
Finally I'd curl back up on the mat,
Life is easy being a cat.

Kelly Myler (11)
Bankfield High School

HOLIDAYS

Going to the airport
Going on the plane
Going on holiday far, far away.
Shall we go to Paris or
Shall we go to Spain or
Shall we go somewhere else where there's lots of rain?
If we go to Paris we'll see lots of sights,
But if we go to Spain we'll get mosquito bites.
Then if we go somewhere it rains we won't be able to play our games.

Kirsty Hunter (11)
Bankfield High School

TODAY I AM CHANGING SCHOOL

Today I am changing school,
I really am nervous,
I'm so excited too.
I hope I find lots of friends.
My best friend is coming and
She is really excited too.
I'm an only child but my
Friend has got a sister.
I don't know if we're in the same
Class but I hope we are.
I'm stepping up to something new
And very big too.
I hope that
Everyone is nice to me because
I'll be nice to them.
A few weeks later
I have made lots of friends,
I never thought I would.
I have a lovely teacher,
She's so kind
And nice.
The best thing ever is that my best friend is
In my class so that's what I'm
Made up with most,
And I think I'm going to be happy.

Nicole Carter (11)
Bankfield High School

THE MEMORIES OF STEAM

Queuing up for a ticket
Bustling crowds, all around
'What is that sound'
Chug; chug; whoosh, whistling wheels
Squealing around
Smoke fills the station
The train pulls in
The crowd moves to the platform
What a din
Scramble on the train
Crowds push in
Find a seat
'What a treat
A window seat'
Woo-woo, the whistle blows
Hear the wheels squeal
As off the train goes
Hedges, trees, streams, we pass
On a journey from the past
We ascend the mountain path
Moaning and groaning the old train puffs
Struggling to keep going
It must, it must.

The top of the mountain is now in sight
Hurry up train
You know I am right
At last we're there
Squealing wheels come to a stop
At last, at last
We're at the top.

Daniel Jones (12)
Bankfield High School

WALKING AROUND

Miaow!
I'm walking around the house,
It's quite a big journey for me,
Maybe I could catch a mouse.
I can handle anything,
I just want to go outside,
I'm only a little kitten,
But my owners won't let me out
So I carry on my journey
All around the house.
Two years later
I've grown up, now I'm going out.
I can't wait to walk about.
Now I'm outside, where should I go?
I know, I'll go up that side of the street.
So I walk up the road having some fun,
Rolling and rolling outside on my own.
I had fun till the end of the day.
Oh my goodness, I've lost my way.
I carried on the road all through the night,
Oh, I didn't half give me a fright and then I stopped.
There I lay down in fright. I was so scared through the night
And as soon as morning came
I was at my front doorstep again.
I scratched the door, my owner let me in,
Ever since then I won't go out
And when there's no sound outside
I know it's night and when night comes I scream and shout and
Then I know that night is here again.

Jessica Hunt (11)
Bankfield High School

UNTITLED

Greasy burgers, sticky fingers
The smell of McDonald's lingers.
Magical, fantastical, favourite things.
Comic books and laser guns
Chicken fried rice and currant buns
Magical, fantastical, favourite things.
Delamere forest on my pedal bike
School comes closer, that's what I like,
Magical, fantastical, favourite things.
Sewing a coat for the winter days
Dreaming for the summer days
And autumn haze.

Andrew Goodier (11)
Cloughwood School

WINTER SCENE

Snow covers the leaves of bracken, feel the winter chill.
Snowmen melt like one single ice cube,
Going without saying goodbye,
My roof is thatched with white, white snow,
Santa rides up in the sky, touching stars that
Shine so high.
With a shout and a laugh and a ho, ho, ho,
Santa delivers his presents so slow.
Over the night Rudolph cries
Covering the skies with a thousand sighs.

Graham White (12)
Cloughwood School

PLAYTHINGS

Volleyball and football
Sweets and beats
Fantastical, magical
These are all my playthings.

Table tennis and Buxton Park
The Menace called Dennis and
A singing lark.
Fantastical, magical
These are all my playthings.

CD discos and yummy crisps
San Francisco and bonfire wisps
Fantastical, magical
These are all my playthings.

The English border and slippery fish
High-pitched recorder and a birthday wish
Fantastical, magical,
These are all my playthings.

William Huxley (12)
Cloughwood School

ALL GOOD THINGS

Chocolate cakes and solar beams
High jump and basketball,
Magical, fantastical
Favourite things.

Bicycles and hockey balls,
Golf and pool
Magical, fantastical
Favourite things.

Football and trampolining,
Cornwall and France,
Magical, fantastical
Favourite things.

Painting and sleeping,
Motorbikes and cars,
Magical, fantastical
Favourite things.

Jonathan Riley (11)
Cloughwood School

FAVOURITE THINGS

Swimming whales and high wind gales
Autumn leaves and hay in bales
Favourite, fantastical
Magical things.

Chips, peas and fish arrive on a dish
A day in bed would be my dearest wish
Favourite, fantastical
Magical things.

Bright brown conkers and knotted strings
Drive you bonkers and other things
Favourite, fantastical
Magical things.

Jet streams and salad creams
Snowy days and Christmas dreams
Favourite, fantastical
Magical things.

Simon Ward (11)
Cloughwood School

ALL GOOD THINGS

Chocolate bars and a summer day,
Zooming cars and the month of May.
Magical, fantastical,
Favourite things.

Crunchy crisps and my brilliant mum,
November mist and holiday fun.
Magical, fantastical,
Favourite things.

Brainy maths and sailing boats,
Leafy paths and nice warm coats.
Magical, fantastical,
Favourite things.

Fishing float and fish and chips,
Castle moats and apple pips.
Magical, fantastical,
Favourite things.

Computer games and swimming pools
Whizzing lanes and diving fools.
Magical, fantastical,
Favourite things.

Matthew Pleavin (11)
Cloughwood School

WONDERFUL THINGS

PlayStations and train stations,
Chippy ships and fizzy pop,
Magical, fantastical, favourite things.

Floating goats and high wind gales,
Chocolate bars and jammy tarts,
Magical, fantastical, favourite things.

Smashing conkers and Delamere forest,
Tangled reels and fishing hooks,
Magical, fantastical, favourite things.

Swimming exhaustion and speedy cars,
Monkeys, hot dogs and treetop birds,
Magical, fantastical, favourite things.

Nick Blezard (12)
Cloughwood School

MY FAVOURITE THINGS

Mars bars and Milky Bars
Neptune and the planet Mars
These are all my favourite things.

Playing football, scoring goals
Playing golf, putting holes
These are all my favourite things.

Christmas trees and carol singers
My dad's keys and chocolate fingers
These are all my favourite things.

Reading poems and good books
Mathematics and girls with looks
These are all my favourite things.

Going to discos to dance all night
The moon and stars that shine so bright
These are all my favourite things.

Listening to my radio, playing it loud
Watching Man Utd listening to the crowd
These are all my favourite things.

Philip Cooper (13)
Cloughwood School

ALL GOOD THINGS

Days in Blackpool and fish and chips,
Ice-cream cool and greasy lips.
Magical, fantastical,
Favourite things.

Chocolate bars and jammy cake,
Racing cars and still blue lakes.
Magical, fantastical,
Favourite things.

Monkeys, hot dogs and flowers, cartoons,
Noisy fairgrounds and floating balloons.
Magical, fantastical,
Favourite things.

Chewy toffee and apple pie,
The smell of coffee and a butterfly.
Magical, fantastical,
Favourite things.

Gareth Lewis (11)
Cloughwood School

FAVOURITE THINGS

Swimming whales and fishermen's sails,
Singing snails and high wind gales,
Magical, fantastical,
Favourite things.

Game Boys and sweets,
Insane boys and treats,
Magical, fantastical,
Favourite things.

Plants and holes,
Ants and moles,
Magical, fantastical,
Favourite things.

Singing lark and top marks,
Swinging park and go carts,
Magical, fantastical,
Favourite things.

Philip Martin (11)
Cloughwood School

MY FAVOURITE THINGS

Computer screen
And army cadets
Tins of beans and a couple of pets

Fireworks flying
Dancers dancing
Tins of beans and a couple of pets

Yorkshire terriers
Computer scanners
Tins of beans and a couple of pets

Rainy night
Bonfire Night
Tins of beans and a couple of pets

Warm slippers
Warm beds
Tins of beans and a couple of pets.

Leslie Rennie (13)
Cloughwood School

UNTITLED

I know where to touch . . .
To make you feel
I know how to hold
So you know
You've experienced a love that is true.
In one night
I share myself with you.

Michael Lord Griffiths (15)
Cloughwood School

A DARKNESS OUT THERE IN HERE

There's a darkness out there,
Darkness,
A darkness in everyone;
In a smiling man,
A laughing child,
That smile hides it,
That laugh hides it,
It's a darkness out there.
In here.
There's a darkness out there,
Darkness,
A darkness in everyone;
From the lovely newborn
To the sweet old pensioner,
Perhaps not so lovely,
Not so sweet,
It's a darkness out there.
In here.

James Byrne (14)
Congleton High School

STRIMMER

I am long, resourceful and strong,
I bend everything to my will,
From the tall grass weeds, which I am designed for,
To the innocent frog,
Whose life I can bring to a standstill,
With one rotation of my strong blade.

I emit sound waves,
As I execute my prey,
Sound waves of great decibels,
Even the MPs complain.

My best companion, the lawn mower,
As it too destroys life,
All it lacks is efficiency,
For it does not have the capability to destroy all life,
Great and small.

Now both my companion and I have silenced,
For a short time at least,
But this I guarantee, to all life around me,
My work is not done,
And my plant victims at least,
Shall grow and strive,
So I may strive to slaughter,
Once more.

Jemma Armitage (16)
Congleton High School

SLAVERY

No money, no freedom,
No time to play.
No siblings, no friends,
They just took me away.

From my parents,
Who loved me,
To this monster,
Who beats me.

Work hard, work long,
Work twenty hours a day.
Go to spend a penny, then
Get back quick without delay.

From my parents,
Who loved me,
To this monster,
Who beats me.

Slave labour, they call it,
But call it what may,
It's not right, it's evil,
Injustice I say.

From my parents,
Who loved me,
To this monster,
Who beats me.

Rebellion, break loose,
Got to get away.
Abscond, time to run,
To where we can play!

From my parents,
Who loved me,
To this monster,
Who beats me.

Get caught, become trapped,
Then get beaten all day.
After cry yourself to sleep,
Only got religion so I pray.

From my parents,
Who loved me,
To this monster,
Who beats me.

No money, no freedom,
No time to play,
You can stop this,
Come help me, I'm not okay!

Joseph Swindells (13)
Congleton High School

MONKEY ON THE LOOSE

Beware, there's a monkey on the loose!
He's big, he's bold and his name is Bruce.
Last week he robbed a bank,
Yesterday he stole an army tank.
He's destroyed half the city,
He's in the bad books with the committee.
If you see him don't approach,
Call the army!
Call the zoo!
But don't let him capture you!

Nicola Beard (12)
Congleton High School

DREAMING

I hear harmony playing a soft minuet,
I see afterlife drifting in the breeze,
But if dreams would last forever,
I think our lives would be perfect.

In the morning I wake to a cloudless sky,
And to hear a sweet bluebird's song,
Then in the middle of a sentence
I stop, to feel a spirit floating by.

That's what I dreamt on Sunday night,
They're strange things, dreams,
And I wonder what I'll dream tonight,
If I have a dream.

Alysa-Jayne Thomas (13)
Congleton High School

THE MONSTER

There's a monster in my wardrobe,
it's all green and slimy.

There's a monster in my wardrobe,
it's smelly and wet.

There's a monster in my wardrobe,
my mummy says there isn't.

There's a monster in my wardrobe,
it's there, it snores very loudly.

And I can't sleep!

There's a monster in my wardrobe,
it's . . .

Susan Bossons (12)
Congleton High School

THE MOON THAT NIGHT

There I stood upon the ground,
Looking up at the moon,
So shiny and round.

A milky white drop
All dappled on top,
With a surface that shines
Like the diamond mines.
In the velvety sky
Up there so high,
The moon that night
So shiny and bright.

As full as a lake after a flood,
As fresh as a tiny pink rosebud.
Balancing so elegantly up there
(Like a ballerina en pointe to be fair).
Inside it made me feel so small,
Wishing again to grow up tall.
It was so high and far away,
I wanted to ask if I may,
Be made a fairy for one eve
And then this earth I would leave,
And fly up to that dream-like sphere
Instead of standing dreaming here.

Gemma Comer (13)
Congleton High School

A Night By The Sea

It was a beautiful sunset at the Menai Straits.
I lay on the sandy beaches watching the ocean waves.
The ocean was dark red from the fading glow of the sun
as it left for another place.
The tide slowly rising, the sea was now at rest.
Then the clouds came,
like a quilt they covered me,
plunging the last glints of the sun into darkness.
There was a noise like a howl from a wolf,
as the waves clashed against the rocks,
the rhythmic sound was restless.
The sea never sleeps.
Eventually light returned, life began again
in a continuous loop until the next night
at the Menai Straits . . .

Andrew Scott (11)
Congleton High School

My Cat Sooty

My cat Sooty is a real big cutie
And purrs all the time.
He's black and white and rather light
And we love him very much.
He loves his food, especially chicken
And afterwards, his lips he can't stop licking.
He's really sweet and cuddly too
and for his nickname we call him Pooh.
He comes in all soggy and wet
And I am very glad to have him for a pet.
He really is a lovely puss and
Would stand all day having a fuss.

Claire Davis (14)
Congleton High School

THE BULLY

The playground was still,
Everything froze,
Not a cough or a sneeze
Or a wiggle of toes.

The dogs have finished barking,
The birds are still too!
Don't get on the wrong side of him,
'Cause he'll find you.

He comes through the main doors,
Stooge by his side,
Most people try
To run off and hide.

Don't beat him at anything,
Maths or hide-and-seek,
As you will be
His punch bag for a week.

Let me give you this advice,
Don't treat him like a lark,
As you will soon learn
His bite is worse than his bark.

Don't mess around with him
Or he'll push you in the gully
And beat you up to smithereens,
As he is the playground bully.

Charlotte Barlow (12)
Congleton High School

STAFFROOM

What is in there?
Two teachers who are turning into aliens?
A spaceship?
Alien food?
Go on, open the door, go on.
No.
That means you're scared.
No I'm not, you are!

So, what's in there?
Stuffed animals?
Rugs made out of bears' fur?
Guns?
Knives,
And real, live bears?
Open that door, or else!
No, we're in enough trouble already.

So what's in there?
A sports car?
A fighting motorbike?
A turbo bike?
Go on, open the door.
No.
Yes.
OK.

He gripped the handle,
Pulled it down and opened the door.
There was a cup of cold tea,
A box of mouldy chocolates,
The cupboard,
Loads of paper,
Empty boxes,
Discarded pens
And not forgetting
The teachers.

Lucy Harding (11)
Congleton High School

HALLOWE'EN

As the ground was haunted by a mist of cloud,
Children pleased with their costumes and proud,
A few girls dressed as Snow White
And boys dressed as horses and knights!
All around pumpkins lit up,
Candy filled in bowls and a cup!
Children knocking on doors for treats,
Candles and pumpkins, little and big.
Madonna dressed up in make-up and a wig,
Little princesses sauntering up and down,
The King of England wearing a crown.
Dracula stabbing his fangs into sweets,
Candy bowls bulging full,
As the night gets dark and dull.
The moon comes out from the misty sky,
As it goes dark, you begin to cry.
Now Hallowe'en is over again,
The ghosts can go home to their haunting den!

Lucy Hodgkinson (11)
Congleton High School

MAZED

Deaf, that's what I am, deaf!
Did I hear the bell go?

The children had deserted me,
The playground was bare,
I could only see in the distance fencing,
Trapping me in.

My heart was pounding,
It wanted to escape.
One pound too hard made me jump,
I scuttled inside.

I'd seen it on the telly, the radio too,
I was standing in a school maze!
I had to find my classroom,
One minute late, two minutes late, three.

I walked calmly one way,
Dead end.
I walked slowly another way,
Dead end.

I walked quickly another way,
Dead end.
I panicked. I'd be late for my *first day!*

I ran down the erm . . . corridor.
I passed Mr Finnigan's room,
Then Mrs Baker's too.

But the only room I couldn't find was
Mrs Teacher's room.
Then just as I was about to give up,
I peered in a room and the room
Was filled with little people.
That was the room for me!

I slowly turned the handle,
Then I walked in.
Googly eyes stared at me.
Me. Why me?

Laura Butler (11)
Congleton High School

FIRST DAY AT SCHOOL

I stood in the hall all alone,
But two girls came up to me, named Alice and Teresa.
They asked me to go and see the King of the Playground,
Who was sat on the throne,
I went and saw the King, he was nice.

We went to the hall for assembly,
Got shouted at by Mr Spink,
He made us laugh so much, we cried.
We then went to our first lesson, which was music with . . .
Mr Spink.
It was so much fun.

The day had finally finished after five long lessons.
It felt like days and days before we had finished.
When I told my mum, she asked
'Are you going back tomorrow?'
I replied 'Of course I am, I love school!'

Alex Bourner (11)
Congleton High School

THE BAD DAY

I don't want to get up, Mum.
But I was up all night.
I'm not going to school, Mum,
My trousers are too tight.
I've got tummy ache, Mum,
Ear ache too,
I've got a sore throat, Mum,
I'm coughing up goo.
I can't walk to school, Mum,
It's cold out there.
OK, I'll walk, Mum,
I don't care.
Sorry I'm late, Miss,
The car broke down.
I can't find my pencil, Miss,
It must have fallen down.
I've forgotten my homework, Miss,
The dog chewed it up.
I can't help it, Miss,
He's only a pup.
I want my tea, Mum,
I'll have it now.
No, Mum,
I'm not eating a cow.
I'm not going to bed, Mum,
I'm not zzzzzzzz . . .

Laura Edwards (11)
Congleton High School

THE LESSON MONSTERS

The lesson monsters,
They're creatures trapped in classrooms behind locked doors.

When we go in, are they going to attack us?
They sound small and slimy.

They hide everywhere in the school,
You can't get away.

There's one in every lesson,
They pick a new person and follow him.

They also like new kids
Not knowing their way along.

They lurk in dark places,
Away from the light.

They're going to get you,
So stay out of the way.

Benjamin Hadwick (12)
Congleton High School

LOVE?

I wonder why he's just a guy,
yet he holds the power to make me cry.
Does this mean that he's the one?
I love him so and now he's gone.
Now he seems so far away.
Will he be mine again some day?

He's so special and in my heart,
I thought we'd be together forever,
So close, but yet so far apart!

I get butterflies when he says my name,
I love him so I wish he'd feel the same.
If this ain't love, answer me this,
Why do I long for his warm, tender kiss?

I ain't one of those girls
Who will give you love for a standard fee.
I told you I loved you
And you laughed at me.
I always dreamed I'd find the perfect lover,
But he turned out to be the same as every other!

Alison Humphries (13)
Golborne High School

THE PETROL BLOCKADE

Roads are quiet,
Blockades are on,
Men are shouting,
'Petrol's gone.'

Shelves are empty,
Shops are full,
Women are shouting,
'Milk's all gone.'

Blockades are over,
Still long queues,
Because of rumours
On the news.

Clare Mills (13)
Golborne High School

I HAVE . . .

I have a next-door neighbour
who is weird in every way.
Her house is blue, her name is Sue,
has teeth full of decay.

I have an older brother
who is out most of the time,
but when he's in, he drinks the gin
and sometimes even wine.

I have a school teacher
who's obsessed with Elton John.
She's always chanting, 'I'm Still Standing'
and what's the other one?

I have a dog called Lucky
who's the best pet in the world.
She has a tail, collects the mail,
I put her hair in curls.

I have a little teddy
who is printed on a kite,
flies in the park, but now it's dark,
I bid you all goodnight!

Kayleigh Prior (13)
Golborne High School

SPACE

Do UFOs really exist?
People say they do.
They fly about the skies at night
And give people such a fright.

Does space really exist?
Scientists say it does,
There are the planets above
And they look down on you.

Why do the stars shine so bright
And yet seem so far away?
Look at the man in the moon high up in the sky,
Shining down upon us. What does he see?

Why are there comets and asteroids in space?
Can't the world just be a perfect place?
They cause so much devastation when they strike,
We must be lucky that they don't hit us.

Claire Singleton (13)
Golborne High School

THE INTERNET

The Internet is a complicated thing,
With all the information you need,
But how to find it is really the problem,
At least it's at rocket speed.

It's marvellous but mainly confusing,
Astounding, yet hard to understand.
The information on it is unbelievable,
What you learn of it is somewhat grand.

All these *www's* take a long time to grasp,
And e-mail addresses too complex for most,
After you've mastered it you can't keep away
And because we've got it we boast.

Now that you understand the Internet,
You decide that you're ready for more.
You're waiting for the new technology,
That's ready to come through that door.

Chris Hide (13)
Golborne High School

DO YOU HATE HIM TOO?

Do you hate him also? I know that I do.
He's 'orrible 'n' nasty and he frightens me too.
He has sharp tools which really hurt
When they dig in your mouth and scrape out all the dirt.
As you sit in 'The Chair' you gaze up his nose,
He advances upon you, the fear inside grows.
Your vision is blurred and all starts to spin,
As he gropes in your mouth and the drilling begins . . .

You start to gag and heave and spit,
The goop in your mouth tastes like grit.
This awful man, what right has he got?
He must be in on an evil plot
To steal your teeth in the dead of the night,
When you can't scream or put up a fight.
I hate this man, I really do.
The dentist; do you hate him too?

Emma Prior (13)
Golborne High School

MY OWN STAR

In a world so dark,
In a sky so high
Above the longest park,
To get up there, I could try.

Near a cloud so white
Was a star so big
Which shines so bright,
I could dance and jig.

And so pleased was I
To see in the sky
This star so white
Make the world so bright.

Excited I was so much,
I was completely tongue-tied.
I could've talked double Dutch
Believe me, for I have not lied.

Now, with much joy,
Without anger or annoy
I can tell the skies
My happiness, secrets and lies.

For now I have found
What I was looking for.
Worth much more than a pound,
A star to tell my problems.
No less, no more.

Laura Mayoh (13)
Golborne High School

SPIDERS

I hate spiders
Big and small,
I hate spiders on my wall.

Large and hairy,
They give me the creeps.
Small and skinny,
They hide in the deeps.

I hate spiders,
Cobwebs 'n' all,
Building them always
In the corners of my wall.

Inside and outside
My window frame,
Oh they really
Are a pain.

I hate spiders
Down plugholes,
I wish I could crush them
With my shoe sole.

I hate spiders,
Big and small.
I hate spiders.
I hate them all!

Catherine Stonier (13)
Golborne High School

THE STORY OF A KITTEN

On January 9th all was quiet,
except for a cat's miaow.
The cat gave birth to three tiny kittens,
although I don't know how.

A white kitten with black spots, a black kitten with white spots
and a little tabby kitten which plays with pans and pots.

All three will go to homes
when they are eight weeks old.
And this you will see
is how my story unfolds.

On the 5th of March I got to choose my kitten.
I chose the white one and you'll see I'm smitten.

I named my kitten Snowy,
and he was very, very small,
and he chases his mouse
round and round the hall.

He loves to be fussed, tickled and cuddled,
but if everyone shouts his name at once he can get muddled.

He is growing up
very, very fast.
Although I knew his being a kitten
would never last.

Snowy really loves me, I really love him back,
he plays outside and catches mice (he's really got the knack!)

I could go on forever,
but I haven't got the time.
And I have told you so much
about the kitten which is mine.

So here the story ends, the story of a kitten
Of which I have said before I'm absolutely *smitten!*

Janine Lawton (14)
Golborne High School

THIS TIME OF YEAR

When you look out in the garden
And you peer up at the trees
You will see the birds now flocking
To fly off overseas.

Leaves are changing colour,
Yellow, red and brown,
Conkers are now ready
To come a-tumbling down.
Berries on the bushes,
Shiny blacks and reds,
Squirrels collecting acorns
To line their winter beds.

Autumn is upon us,
The nights are drawing in.
The wind is turning colder,
Soon winter will begin.

Keith Gibson (13)
Golborne High School

THE VAMPIRE

He moves like the wind,
He moves in silence,
Never looking back,
Getting ready to pounce.

He sees his prey
And corners it with ease.
A rustle comes from behind and he turns to see
What looks like a bigger animal than he.

A struggle takes place and he runs,
Runs so far he may not be seen again.
Is he hurt?
Well, he does not care, for his hunger means much more.

In the corner of his eye he sees a movement, and
His hunger strikes once again.
He yelps in pain as his stomach churns,
As he fears his prey might hear.

A young girl of about sixteen is on the edge of the road.
She looks as if she is waiting, waiting for something to pounce.
He creeps up behind her and she turns to see . . .
A vampire, waiting to feed!

He does not know she is the slayer,
She has no fear inside,
For all of the demons she has ever slain,
This, she thought, would be the easiest of them all.

His eyes meet hers and a wrench of pain
Shoots through his body like one thousand knives.
The eyes that were red are now yellow and
She has set his demon soul free.

He no longer sucks blood from innocent people's necks,
As he knows *she* patrols the town.
He knows he should not, but he cannot help himself,
He has fallen in love with this girl.

Louise Northey (13)
Golborne High School

ENGLISH POEMS

Once upon a time,
No that's not right.
If I read it in public,
there'd be no one in sight.

The poems I write are so . . .
Really bad.
The amount of rhyme used can be really . . .
Quite sad.

Here is my poem,
You can hear it right now.
Because I have just finished,
Though I'm not sure how . . .

Well what do you think,
Do you think that it's good?
Because I've just achieved something
I didn't know I could.

In fact no,
I think that it's great.
Well I'd better end now,
It's getting late.

Mark O'Brien (13)
Golborne High School

THE WITCH

The lonely witch of Minstrels Wood
had been cast out of the village even though she was good.
She lives in a cottage that's falling to pieces,
'One day I'll have my revenge,' she whispers.

She only goes out when the moon is full,
Gathers up toadstools, frogspawn and wool.
Puts them in a cauldron, mutters some words,
Opens her spell book and stirs and stirs.

She picks up a ladle and dips it in,
Pours the murky brown liquid into a bottle of gin.
She hobbles outside with her goods in a bag,
Waits by the roadside and watches a stag.

As the travellers go by,
She mumbles 'Come die.'
Puts on a smile,
Lays out her stock and sells drinks by the pile.

As she's walking home she can still hear the screams
Of innocent people having terrible dreams.
Their lives have become a permanent nightmare,
As she closes the door and stares into the fire.

Naomi Allen (14)
Golborne High School

HOMEWORK

We all have homework,
It makes you think.
Sometimes it's easy,
Sometimes it stinks.

Most of the time
It is hard,
So I do it
In the school yard.

My mum makes a fuss
When she finds out
I've done it
On the school bus.

I always get Cs and Ds,
I'm sure the teachers
Don't
Like me.

Science and English are the worst,
With maths
Coming a close
Third.

If I don't do my homework,
I will end up in school detention,
For one long hour when I could be at home,
Listening to the radio and singing a song.

Scott Tither (13)
Golborne High School

THE HAUNTED HOUSE

This house is haunted by a ghost.
No one has ever seen him,
But every one who passed this house
Will be left in no doubt of his existence!

This house is haunted by a ghost.
No one has ever seen him.
Over the fields, up the hillside,
Is where this house stands.

This house is haunted by a ghost.
No one has ever seen him.
If you're brave enough to open the door,
You'll seek to find a scary roar!

This house is haunted by a ghost.
No one has ever seen him.
If you're brave enough to explore this house,
Beware. Beware, boo! Will be your next scare.

This house is haunted by a ghost.
No one has ever seen him.
Go up the stairs if you dare
And where, oh where?
You're not there!

Craig Thompson (13)
Golborne High School

WINTER IS NO MORE

I am sitting in my bedroom,
Gazing through the frosty window,
I see the houses and roads I know so well,
Coated in a thick layer of snow,
White and pure, like silk,
And icicles are hanging from the wet, cold window sill,
The trees are bearing nothing but their branches.

The fire is cosy and warm where I am sat,
But outside, no, not out there,
In the lonely village
It is cold, icy cold.
I cannot bear it, but oh,
How I wish I could be out there,
I could be out there, but I am alone.

Alone, I cannot be with the snow,
I cannot be with the ice,
If I were not alone, I wouldn't be sitting here now,
I would be out in the cold night air,
Gliding across the ice
Like a bird flying through the skies.
Winter would be my companion . . . if only.

But it's too late. It's impossible,
Spring has arrived; the snow has disappeared,
All I can do is hope
And hope, and hope for another chance,
Another chance to be out there
In a magical world of my own,
But winter is no more.

Lauren Foster (13)
Golborne High School

WHAT TO DO!

'Right class, a poem today.'
I thought 'No way.'
I think poems are grim,
Every idea I have goes in the bin.
I could do one about the Tazmanian Devil
Or even the footballer, Gary Neville.
I could do a non-rhyming one, that would be easy,
Though those ones are always sleazy.
I could write one about a surfer on the beach,
Or possible a bloodsucking leech.
I just can't think of anything to do,
I bet no one else wanted to do the poem too.
Now I have no room on my paper,
Maybe I'll think of one later.

Kyle Simm (13)
Golborne High School

THE YEAR 2000!

The year 2000 has begun,
Which everyone thought would never come.
It's a year that people want to celebrate,
It's changed so many things - even the date!
When the clock struck past midnight on New Year's Eve
There was so much excitement that people received,
After all - it's such a special year,
It makes people want to shout and cheer!
At first it all seemed really strange,
I couldn't get used to things that had changed,
But now I'm glad - this year's been fun,
So I'd better make the most of what's left,
Before it's 2001!

Rachel Grimshaw (13)
Golborne High School

FEAR FEN

I speak to you of Fear Fen
The deep and dark and dusky den
Of It that lives to prey on men
Who stumble on the moor.

Not many speak of It for fear
That It may come and slash, here and there
In families young and old
Killing with the teeth and claws so cold.

Now tell a story of a victim do I
His name was John Mugi
He was a loner, dull and groaning
But rather taken to lonely roaming.

John did not heed the warnings of men
That It would see him stumble on the fen, and kill him in a fight
But John was an arrogant man and said he would go
And kill this It and take its head for all to see, and him to show.

But we found him late that Sunday night after mass was done
A torn, and ripped, and slashed up body draped out by It to show
That roamers who do stumble or try to kill for show
Won't last that long on Fear Fen, they will just have to go!

Now speak not I of Fear Fen
That horrid, haggled, hairy hive
For all clever men who do fear It
Will say It is alive!

Joshua Felton (13)
Golborne High School

TO GRANDAD

Hello special Grandad,
You really are the best;
I hope you're happy in Heaven,
You really deserve a rest.

We all really love you,
And that you mustn't forget;
I know you're here, just can't see you,
I've not got used to that yet.

To your family you were devoted,
We were loved, spoilt and looked after;
One thing I would love to hear again
Is your unique, contagious laughter.

You were always there for me
Whenever I felt down;
You always managed to cheer me up,
You got rid of every frown.

The past three years have been awful;
I seem to attract bad luck;
My nana and grandad have gone;
Two special people death took.

You told me so many stories,
At photos I loved to look.
You told me of childhood memories
Of which I could write a book.

People say that time heals,
It's not true, things get worse every day;
I miss you more as time passes,
To stop this there isn't a way.

But Grandad, I'll have to go now,
I'll see you again someday;
Remember I really love you,
I think of you every day.

Jenna Rutter (13)
Golborne High School

PARENTS

They listen at your bedroom door,
While one of them begins to snore,
They glare at the floor and say that's a disgrace,
Come on put everything back in its place!

They'll lurk round the corner, if you are late,
They even embarrass you in front of your mates!
Everywhere you go they know you are there,
That's enough to pull out your hair.

It's like being followed by a big pair of eyes,
They should take up jobs as top secret spies!
Strolling around looking not one bit suspicious,
You might even say they were acting malicious.

They would clamber up trees and hide behind walls,
They'd actually pretend they were looking at stalls,
They ring on your mobile, it's time to come home,
I've got to go into the dreaded doom dome!

But there is one good thing to come out of all this!
The love and attention that we all would miss,
The time and affection that is spent on us dearly,
Hey Mum and Dad, we love you *really!*

Hannah Lowe (13)
Golborne High School

MUSIC

M aking music enlightens my brain,
    Mozart, Beethoven, Grieg, and Bach
    Made classical music through the ages.
    As I turn the pages in my book,
    I have a quick look,
    The bass clef and the melody look really good to me,
    The moment I strike a note my head is in the clouds.
U niversally music is well known,
    From the harmony to the bone.
    The rhythm, dynamics and the pitch
    All have an important part in music.
    Soon the beat kicks in and so does the violin.
S mooth, soft, soothing music,
    Clears our problems away.
    The notes ring in my ears,
    The keys bright and crisp.
    Octave high, octave low,
    Playing fast, playing slow.
I nstruments vary from strings to brass,
    Brass to strings,
    The saxophone sounds smooth,
    The piano sounds high-pitched and well tuned.
    Sharps and flats all present,
    A wonderful piece played by a wonderful musician.
C laps and applause break out,
    The orchestra has finished,
    On comes the encore.
    Soon the music slows down,
    Dying, dying away,
    Until the music is gone.

Sarah Wilde (13)
Golborne High School

A SINGER'S FANTASY

All lights go off but the spotlight,
Hot, bright, waiting.
A hushed silence creeps and spreads,
About the candlelit room,
A thousand eyes are gazing,
Their owners anticipating,
Waiting for the show to begin.

My butterflies turn to snakes,
Fighting and biting inside me.
Not a single curl can escape the ribbon.
Matching my black sparkling dress,
Black strap heels imprison my ankles.
My face is professionally made up.
I feel ready, yet unprepared for the night ahead.

I'm introduced to the crowd,
As I step on the stage.
The band begins to play the first song,
A slow, steady ballad.
Maybe next I'll sing an up or mid tempo,
All I know, as I stand in the spotlight,
Years of dreams and fantasy have come true.

Lisa Quinn (13)
Golborne High School

THE KING AND QUEEN ON HALLOWE'EN

In Spooksville on Hallowe'en
There is a shudder as out comes the Queen
She lives in the mansion on top of the hill
The King, her husband is writing her will
You see he is planning to kill

The King is desperate for her money
He has a strong addiction to honey
He likes to make traps to catch witches
On Hallowe'en the honey makes them itchy

The King's plan has backfired
The Queen is talking to the witch that she has hired
She has planned the same
She wants to win the game

Then their son comes in
And says that he will commit a sin
He draws a gun and points it to the sun
After that all was still on Hallowe'en.

Sarah Griffiths (13)
Golborne High School

WHY?

Why
did you do it to me
the way you did it, why?
I'll never know!

Why
you said yes
and then you said no, why?
I'll never know!

Why
won't you tell me
what have I done wrong, why?
I'll never know!

Why
you did it again
for a second time and why?
I'll never know.

Elizabeth Riley (13)
Golborne High School

TEACHERS

Deep in the dark murky depths of the school,
Lies a monster to shame any demon or ghoul.
In a horrid French room it does lurk,
Setting painful homework.

In case the answer is unable to reach ya,
The topic of my poem is called a teacher.
Not just any old Sir or Miss,
This one teaches us English.

It makes us read and other types of torture,
Once you've been teachered there's nothing to cure ya.
They make you eat toxins and drink cyanide,
When it comes to lunch time I'd advise you to hide.

It sits its victims down in seats made of plastic,
And tells us of punctuation and things just as drastic.
Shakespeare, riddles and how to use a noun,
Inspire the whole class to want to leave town.

Melissa Richards (13)
Golborne High School

THE CREATURE

The ocean roaring as it smashes against rocks,
Out in the distance a tiny head pops up to say 'Hello,'
I can see a whole family of them weaving through the waves,
Jumping through the waves, jumping higher and higher,
Can you tell what they are yet?

The wind brushing past me, leaving me all cold and shivery,
More swimming past our boat as smoothly as they glide
        through the water,
I am really amazed to see these wonderful creatures,
Dancing through the crashing waves!
Can you tell what they are yet?

The sea is calming, the air is silent, peace at last,
They are surrounding our boat now,
These are the very best animals in the world,
The sun setting on the horizon, I wish I never had to leave.
These wonderful animals are *dolphins.*

Natasha Evans (11)
Hartford High School

MY PONY CANDY

Far in the hills of Devon,
A small pony grazes,
I watch him with fascination,
He is young and playful.

In his stable that night,
I notice a lump on his face.
Hurriedly I phone the vet,
Pony's eyes are dull and sad.

The next day at the stable,
He is weak and feeble on the floor.
He rests his head on my lap,
Slowly he closes his eyes and is still.

I remember him when he was born,
A young foal at his mother's side.
My pony has gone,
But I will always remember him.

Hollie Lunn-Smith (11)
Hartford High School

THE HAUNTED CHURCH

T   he hall of the church
H   aunts you all the time
E   verywhere in there you go

H   all of church is all they say
A   nd go in there and waste away!
U   nderneath the floorboards
N   orman finds a body
T   he ghost is behind him
E   lectric lights go dim
D   oor slams, he turns round

C   overed in sheets
H   e is glowing in the dark
U   h! No it's a ghost
R   rrr! Went the ghost
C   ringing I am in fright
H   ey! Why can't it be good at night?

Andy Oakes (12)
Hartford High School

HAUNTED HOUSE OF HORROR

H aunted house sits on a hill,
A nd every Hallowe'en
U nexplained things happen
N ow I see a ghost, then it disappeared
T hen once again I saw another
E verywhere I look
D emons are there

H orror is in the air
O h, I see a ghost with hair
U nusual things I see
S cary as the ghost
E ither I stay or run
S piders on the ground as well.

Emily Merriman (11)
Hartford High School

THE MYSTERIOUS WALKER

As the rain fell heavily,
The ghost swept quickly,
Searching, looking, waiting to see,
Where his friend could be.

He wandered carefully,
But gracefully,
Waiting impatiently,
And then finally . . .

He looked upon the horizon,
Frightened and nervous,
He saw waiting, walking, running . . .

Melissa Catherine Humphries (11)
Hartford High School

THE HAUNTED HOUSE

The broken windows, dangerous and sharp,
The spooky music, probably made by a harp.
The ghostly face behind the door,
And not only that but there's lots more . . .

The wood, of the house, rotten and soggy,
The weather, outside, cold and foggy.
The bats wildly flew out,
Of the old tree which caused me to scream, no doubt.

The night has just turned black,
But then I spotted a sack.
Then, something came out,
I couldn't tell what it was but it began to shout!

Dasha Beynon (11)
Hartford High School

CATS AND A DOG

C   uddly and cute
A   re my cats
T   hey can be terrible
S   ometimes

A   lso I will be getting a
N   ew
D   og

A   lsation or what I don't care

D   ogs are playful and jump
O   ver things
G   ood or bad they are cute.

Daniel Dobell (11)
Hartford High School

MY FRIEND, THE DOLPHIN

The gleaming sun sparkles on the waves,
My rowing boat sways to and fro,
The sea laps against my feet,
I feel calm just like the sea.

Under the water a friendly creature plays a game,
Its forever smiling face looks up to my boat,
The creature swims around me,
He feels cheeky and mischievous.

Back in my boat I wait in the moonlight,
Waiting for my friend to come,
My big, grey friend leaps out of the tropical sea,
Says hello in a high-pitched voice
And leaves me waiting once more.

Catherine Davenport (12)
Hartford High School

THE SCREAM

Creeping down the corridor
Sending a shiver down your spine
A quick shock and your heart is beating fast
Making the hair on your neck stand up.
Suddenly a scream.
Ah!
        Ah!
                Ah!
                        Ah!

Garreth Davies (11)
Hartford High School

IS THIS A DREAM, OR AM I DEAD?

As I got out of my bed, the clock struck midnight.
I felt a presence before me.
The smell was putrid, I couldn't see a thing.
My body was floating above me,
And my head was on the floor.

I've never felt like this before,
Empty, lifeless and transparent.
I float along like a breath of chilled air,
Disappearing through doors as though they're not there.

My ghostly body feels chilled and cold,
Where am I, my mind's a blank.
No thoughts or ideas cross my head,
Will I ever wake up, is this a dream or am I dead?

Laura Mercer (12)
Hartford High School

THE RUSTLING IN THE BUSHES

It was the dead of the night and the moon was as full as an orange,
And I was stood in a misty graveyard,
When all was still except for a rustling in the bushes,

I jumped and it sent a shiver up my spine,
I didn't know what to do, should I stay
And see what it is or should I go?

I walked up to where the rustling came from,
I slipped my hand in the bushes,
And there rustling for worms was a *hedgehog*!

Heather Greenwood (11)
Hartford High School

THE WITCH

In the middle of the dark and gloomy wood,
That was where she was stood,
That old and ugly hag,
With her black, leather bag!

Casting her evil spells,
Like making flowers into bells,
Out of her wand came the sparks,
That make children fall over in parks!

Her face with warts,
And in her hair were all sorts,
Standing in the woods, next to the ditch,
Was that smelly, small, sad *witch!*

Nicola Buckley (11)
Hartford High School

A POEM ABOUT WITCHES

Witches are ugly, witches are warty,
Mostly their spells are evil and naughty,
Familiars they have can bring them good luck,
And whilst making spells they help them to cook,
Every witch thinks they've got good looks,
They spend all their time just reading from spell books,
They have crooked big noses and wear pointed hats,
Nearly every witch has a sleek black cat,
Why are witches so naughty,
No one knows, they're just very warty.

Ben Walton (12)
Hartford High School

FLYING HAGS

Witches, witches, everywhere, old and grey with curly hair,
Flying around on crooked old sticks,
Casting spells on poor innocent people,
Curled up and sat beside them are their cats hanging on
                                 for their nine short lives,
Crashing and banging everywhere,
There go the hogs in the air,
Mumbling spells and cracking horrible jokes to the poor
                                 old friendly folk,
Witches, witches, everywhere, doing dares that would raise our hairs,
As day breaks they fly home to their lairs before anyone sees
                                 what they really are!

Ben Ditchburn (12)
Hartford High School

WITCHES' TALE

W et wailing witches fly up into the sky, cackling to
     their black evil cats,
I nto the night comes a black fright, to the amazement
     of a green hairy monster,
T he truth is this, the witches' spells lie on a page open wide,
C auldrons boil into the night, red-hot flames crackle with lots of light,
H owling cats keep you up all night, evil, growling, scratches, bites,
E arthquaking laughs and hair like rats' tails with long pointed noses,
S ticking out warts on her feet, nose and more as she slowly, slowly,
     puts her head down to rest, everyone is happy as the dawn
     will shortly break.

Vanessa Cooper (12)
Hartford High School

LIBER MORTIS

As the dead rise
In their rotting clothes,
Their blood is lost,
As time slowly goes.

Their weapons rusty
And the blades are weak,
Their eyes are empty,
They are decaying freaks.

They drag on weakly
Under their master's eye,
Their minds are lost,
After all of them died.

They limp on slowly,
Weapons on standby,
At their master's word,
The others will die.

Daniel Sutton (12)
Hartford High School

THE GRAVEYARD

I was in a graveyard,
The clock struck midnight,
The thunder was so loud it shook the trees,
The smell of death hung in the air,
An owl hooted in the distance,
I started walking but my body was just standing there,
I was dead.

Jamie Comley (11)
Hartford High School

MATHS, ISN'T IT BORING?

Maths, isn't it boring?
What's going on with x, y and z?
Whoever invented tests, I don't like,
Ruler, compass, calculator, gibberish,
Mathematicians are brainy but who would want to be one?
Not me!
My maths teacher says draw a bar chart in pencil and then write in pen,
But the only thing across my page is Tipp-Ex!
Maths, isn't it boring?
But without maths where would we be?
We wouldn't know how tall we are, or how much sugar to put in cakes,
And we wouldn't have bridges,
How would the nurse take our blood pressure!
And forget about computer games!
Okay, maybe maths is important,
But maths, isn't it boring?

Alison Telford (12)
Hartford High School

THE WITCHES' BREW

Huge black cauldron, skinny cats,
cackling witches with pointy hats.
Spells and potions on the boil,
then they add some caster oil.
Eye of newt and a big frog's liver,
a slimy eel from the bottom of the river.
Laughing and dancing around the pot,
the flames are high, it's getting hot.
Time to cast that evil spell.
The Devil's waiting, you're going to *Hell.*

Gemma Dutton (12)
Hartford High School

DEATH

Are witches ugly, horrid and sly,
Through the dark, lonely night on their brooms do they fly,
With their familiar by their side they think they have nothing to lose,
But if they get seen it is really bad news,
They will be put on trial in front of the town,
And thrown in the river where they will probably drown,
But if they don't the townspeople know they're right,
And they will be burned, not a nice sight.

Jamie Glaze (12)
Hartford High School

THE DERELICT HOUSE

Pushing through the broken door
Entering into the old, derelict house.
The stairs are like the pathway of doom
And the chair in the corner is like a bag of rags.
The smell is like the smell of rotting mice
And the floorboards have holes in like the craters in the moon.

Rebecca Smith (13)
Hartford High School

THE WITCH HUNT

I glide through the air on my tattered old broom,
I am racing to hide and get away from my doom,
If they find me I will be drowned,
I can't let this happen,
I mustn't make a sound!

Ben Aucamp (12)
Hartford High School

DEATH

Innocent women are drowned
Because of pathetic people's lies,
Beautiful cats owned by them
Result in them being accused.
They suffer when neighbours call
Them names and bang on the weak
And innocents' doors.

Syd Blake (13)
Hartford High School

PAUPER

P eople shout unkind abuse at me
A nd beat me up
U sually they chant my name
'P auper! Pauper!' is what they say
E qual is what we should be
R ight, it's about time I take action.

Andrew Smith (14)
Hartford High School

THE SUNSET

The sunset spreads across the sky like a red rose just ripe.
The sunset is like my red lips shining in the light.
The sunset's red glow spreads across to the other side of the world
Like a red sheet covering the sky.

Jade Wilkinson (12)
Hartford High School

A FAMOUS PERSON

If he was a piece of furniture he would be an oak table, well built,
If he was a toy he would be a walkie talkie because he is
                                    always shouting at his team-mates,
If he was a fruit or vegetable he would be a pear because he is
                                    good for his team,
If he was a colour he would be gold because he is very rich,
If he was a musical instrument or sound he would be a
                        microphone because his voice is like one,
If he was a country he would be Denmark because he plays for
                                    them in football.
If he was a piece of clothing he would be a pair of goalkeeper gloves,
If he was an animal he would be a deer because he has quick reactions.

Matthew Didsbury (12)
Hartford High School

THE OLD HOUSE

The derelict house is as old as Methuselah.
It is as dark as a piece of coal
And as dirty as a pig in a mud bath.
On the mantelpiece the dust is as thick as the Lord Of The Rings.
The white sheets are as discoloured as a tramp's teeth;
The floorboards are as creaky as a spring in a chair;
And the windows are as misty as the fog in the morning.
The stairs are as fragile as somebody with brittle bones.
Spiders' webs dominate the house like a king with his kingdom.

Craig Thomson (12)
Hartford High School

A WORLD WITHOUT LOVE

The clouds float away,
The flowers droop,
The leaves fall,
The animals flee
The mountains crumble,
The wind howls,
The stars vanish,
The sun bursts.
The sea dries up,
The moon cries,
The river shrivels up and dies,
The sky falls,
The Earth trembles,
And all because love has ceased.

Claire Bagnall (12)
Hartford High School

WITCHCRAFT

W icked witches cackle as 12 o'clock strikes
I   n deep, dark places lie those who are evil
T   ortured as they are accused of witchcraft
C   ats and bones lie in the haunted room alone
H   idious warts and spots like bursting balloons
C   reeping around, looking for dead bodies
R   acing to their death as they are sent to the ducking stool
A   round the lightless streets lie creeping spiders
F   oul old hags making spells around the cauldron
T   aking the poor innocent people to their death.

Josh Stokes (12)
Hartford High School

A TEACHER

If she was a piece of furniture she would be a couch because
she is laid back.
If she was a toy she would be a jack-in-a-box because she is full
of surprises.
If she was a fruit she would be a strawberry because of her size.
If she was a colour she would be yellow because she is always happy.
If she was a musical instrument she would be a harp because
she never shouts.
If she was a country she would be France, well known.
If she was a piece of clothing she would be hipsters because
she is casual.
If she was an animal she would be a cat.

Caroline Scott (12)
Hartford High School

MY LONG SIMILE - BABY

Every day I woke up peacefully
Like a flower blooming.
But when the baby came
It's waking me up at 4 o'clock,
Like a lorry driver on an early morning shift.
When my mum hears him cry
She's over there
Quicker than a blink.
But I know deep down in my heart
I love him
Like all my friends rolled into one.

Tom Lightfoot (12)
Hartford High School

My Descriptive Poem

Inside the circus Big Top is a hullabaloo of noise.
The Ringmaster cracks his whip like a shot from a gun.
The band strikes up the music for the start of the show.
The clowns take up their places like puppets on string.
Elephants trumpet their entrance to the enthusiastic crowd.
Acrobats swing through the air like birds swooping on their prey.
Horses prance in like dainty ballerinas doing their routine.
Lions prowl the perimeter like vultures circling their next meal.
The crowd awaits the grand finale like eager children
                            waiting for Christmas.
The crowds depart and leave the circus Big Top seating area
                            looking like a landfill site.

Andrew Timmis (12)
Hartford High School

The Brain Monster

It's white and gooey and it feasts on brain,
It creeps around the garden when the lights are about to fade,
It seeks an animal with a lovely, juicy brain.
His eyes are wide and can see for miles,
His eyes come up on his prey and prepares to pounce,
It jumps up high over the fence and sticks out its claws.
They sink right down through the skull and the brain oozes out,
He licks it up from off the floor and hides the body deep,
Then scurries off to the garden shed for a good night's sleep!

Jonnie Crawshaw (12)
Hartford High School

THE FUNFAIR

The rollercoaster starts up, it's too late to get off now.
Up and up you go and then down,
the wind hits you in the face like a punch.
Then it slows down when you start to go up the next hump
it seems like a hill but then you start to curve and curl like a snake
through the sands of a desert.
Until you stop abruptly:
like you just hit the end of the universe.

Tom Mitchell (13)
Hartford High School

CASTAWAY

I am lonely and depressed, everybody is tight.
Teased because I am different and because I am not white.
I feel isolated from the world, like nobody cares.
Just walking innocently but people snigger and stare.
Nobody knows the person I am inside.
Because they don't, they make me want to hide.

Emma Collinge (13)
Hartford High School

BUDDY

B   for bullied
U   for unsure
D   for depressed
D   for different
Y   for you're a victim.

Tiffany Beattie (13)
Hartford High School

DESTRUCTION

Gusting wind whistled around the woods
and the branches bent like slender arms,
as the storm raged through.

The wheat shimmered in great waves
of light across the field.

Birds were fighting against walls of current
bursting from the eye of the storm.

The rain leapt up as it punched the ground,
water grenades exploding on impact.

A solitary tree, shook with fear
and its life was ended as it fell with a crash.

A lash of white electricity, stabbed the earth,
then steam rose up from the wound.

Holly Moncrieff (15)
Hartford High School

WITCHES AT NIGHT

W itches come out when it gets dark
I t's the bewitching hour when dogs dare not bark
T he witches mix their potions and brews
C auldron's boil while they exchange news
H allowe'en is their favourite night
E very human should stay out of sight
S o please be quiet, leave them alone, you'll be quite safe
  if you stay at home.

Kirsty Eyres (12)
Hartford High School

THE MONSTER

I lay awake in bed last night
Too scared to move at all
Too afraid to go to sleep
Or shout for help
And bang on the wall

Because the monster would eat me
If it saw me there
I slid under my cover
And cuddled my teddy bear

Shadows on the windowpane
Cutting in through the light
Were like a scary face
Nothing in this world
Like the human race
The evil in its eyes
Held me transfixed
And neutralised
In horror
Would I wake up
When tonight
Became tomorrow
All at once
I heard a scream
And I slowly opened my eyes
Was it all really a dream
The monster was gone
And I was alone
With teddy sitting on my head.

Mark Brown (13)
Hartford High School

THE SHIP WRECKER

A head the size of a small child,
A body the size of two horses,
If you want to be safe for a while,
Don't go in too deep in the sea where its home is.

It lives around small volcanoes,
It lives on people on ships,
It is dangerous, everyone knows,
It can destroy ships like pips.

Although this creature to some ships,
Is pretty small and weak,
But it's got some amazing tactics,
To sink ships into the deep.

It's got three bone spikes on its neck,
Four legs and a lethal tail,
And it's got fins on its bony back,
And nothing on it is frail.

Its got a head that looks like it's upside-down,
And flippers that look like big leaves,
And its got gills so it will never drown,
And lungs so it could leave.

But however mean and terrible,
This creature seems to you,
If you saw it and lived to tell the tale,
You would be amazed at all the colours.

I was!

Joseph Haslehurst (12)
Hartford High School

THE CREATURE

He's out there, he's out there
Looming in the swampy water
A noiseless atmosphere
Isolated from all society

He's out there, he's out there
Mysterious, green and slimy
Surfacing only to eat any humans
Invading his territory

He's out there, he's out there
Two glaring eyes shining
Bright orange in the murky night

He's out there, he's out there
Eating through his scaly arms
Chomping with his sharp, pointed teeth.

Laura Fuller (12)
Hartford High School

DEATHLY GIRL

The deathly girl wonders by
Everything she touches turns white with death
The deathly girl is white in the face
She has lumps in her head
Her purple coat ready to catch us
To torture us till we die
Everyone dreading the day when she comes
They all know what she's there for
To kill!

Anna Palfreyman (12)
Hartford High School

GREEN MOLLIE THE MONSTER

Green Mollie the monster in my garden,
Staring from my tree,
Why do you look so long and hard
When you are looking at me?

Your eyes are as dark as holly,
Of sycamore are your horns,
Your bones are made of elder-branches,
Your teeth are made of thorns.

Your head is made of ivy leaves,
Of bark are your dancing shoes,
And evergreen and green are your jacket,
Your skin and your toes.

Green Mollie the monster
Get down from my tree
Turn that way and get out of my garden
Straight away because you look very ugly to me.

Kelly Thompson (12)
Hartford High School

ZAKEKIMON

Darkness falls across the land
The midnight hour, close at hand
He stalks in search of blood
To terrorise your neighbourhood
And though it cannot be found
By a soul, getting down
You will face the hounds of hell
And rot inside a corpsing shell.

Elliott Baron (12)
Hartford High School

JUST BECAUSE I'M BLACK

Just because I'm black
I'm picked on in school
Just because I'm black
People to me are cruel.

Just because I'm black
It's just not fair
Just because I'm black
I could be murdered any time.

Just because I'm black
People say I commit crime
Just because I'm black
People say I should go back where I came from.

Just because I'm black
I'm disrupted from work
Just because I'm black
People can't accept me for who I am.

Alex Rashid (13)
Hartford High School

MONSTERS

M onsters are horrible, mouldy and slimy
O thers can be hairy, green and gruesome
N ot a lot of monsters are very nice
S omeone ought to put a smile on its face
T ough or weak, they're still horrid things
E ven though you may not think
R eally do you think that monsters are friendly
S omehow I think you must be crazy.

Zoe Quilty (12)
Hartford High School

DO YOU KNOW HOW IT FEELS?

Do you know how it feels
When the brightest day turns into the darkest night?
I do.

Do you know how it feels
To wish you were different?
I do.

Do you know how it feels
When the happiest memory turns into the saddest of thoughts?
I do.

Do you know how it feels
When your life falls apart?
I do.

Do you know how it feels
To be treated the same as everyone else?
I don't, I'm black.

Eilidh McCallum (13)
Hartford High School

MY MEMORIES

M y first time on the beach letting the sand curl around my toes.
E xcitement when a horse gallops across a dewy field,
M emories of when I first saw the snow fall,
O verexcitement when I won my first competition,
R ain splashing on my coat, as I run to school,
I   n the middle of reading my first book,
E ndless beating of drums,
S oft touch of my dog when she's just been washed.
   I will never forget these memories.

Emma Sherwood (11)
Hartford High School

Outcast

Everyone else has friends,
They aren't lonely,
Everyone else fits in,
They aren't different,
Everyone else looks down on me,
Why am I an outcast?

Everyone else is content,
They aren't scared,
Everyone else belongs,
They aren't isolated,
Everyone else is a persecutor,
Why am I victim?

Everyone else is happy,
They aren't depressed,
Everyone else is rich,
They aren't poor,
Everyone else is white,
Why am I black?

Rachel Gilmour (13)
Hartford High School

Witch

Wicked witch with pointed hats,
Warty witch with big black cat,
Into the night on their brooms they ride,
Hoping to be the wizard's bride,
Into the coven they go to meet,
And stirring the cauldron and feeling the heat.

Ricky Jones (12)
Hartford High School

ON THAT DAY

On that day
A school day
I stole £5

On that day
A school day
My mum cried

On that day
A school day
I felt guilty

On that day
A school day
My mum left home

On that day
A school day
My life ended.

Martin Smith (14)
Hartford High School

BEING ME

B   eing me, it's so unfair
E   very day it's me that gets picked on
I   'm the odd one out bringing my books in a carrier bag
N   obody likes me except Julius and Charmain
G   roves and Siddell call me names all the time

M   y trousers are too small and my sweaters are too tight
E   veryone in our class turn their noses up at me.

Lisa Goodrich (13)
Hartford High School

DO YOU KNOW HOW IT FEELS?

Do you know how hard it is to
have very few friends and to be
the only ones to be coloured?

Do you know how it feels
to be shouted at?

Do you know how it feels
to be called names?

Do you know how hard it feels
not to fit in?

Do you know how hard it is
to hear racist jokes?

Do you know we only
have one friend?

Do you know it's Buddy?

How would you feel
in our situation?

We will fight it till the end.
Would you?

Oliver Newman (13)
Hartford High School

IF ONLY I HAD A FRIEND

Here I am without a friend,
Knowing how early my life will end,
Living in fear,
Hate is all I hear,
If only I had a friend,

Cruelty reflected on my bruised face,
While I'm stuck in this popularity race.
We shed a tear,
My mum's not here,
If only I had a friend.

Andrew Morgan (13)
Hartford High School

THE STORM

The distant sky vanished quickly as the black clouds joined
                                                    like a jigsaw.
The immense roar of thunder echoed over the mountains and
                                                    into the horizon.
The sun disappeared as the first raindrops broke from their
                                        charcoal homes.
Twisting rapidly as they descend,
Bombarding the trees and lakes
A bear cub sprints for shelter and the sky is lit by a beam
                                        of fluorescent lightning.
The trapped souls scream from the deserted woods
As the galloping wind dodges every tree with precision before
                                    shooting over the patchwork fields
Leaving the grass dazzled in a whirlpool of wind and mystery.
The valley becomes still and quiet.
The leaves land and a faint chirp can be distinguished.
As it gets louder the velvet black jigsaw is snatched by a touch
                                        of scorching sunlight.
The river flashes its silver water as the sun beams off the pebbles.
The clouds retreat and the sky regains its territory.
A great hawk flies over, screaming the good news.
All that can be seen of the cloud is its evil smile spread across the sky.
The valley will be safe until the next violent storm.

Andrew Logan (15)
Hartford High School

MEMORIES

Many memories go through my head
A few of my favourites are
The way chocolate, smooth and succulent, dribbles in my mouth,
The way smooth soup slips down my throat,
I love a can of Coke sizzling in my face,
I love the way milkshake tickles my tastebuds,
The sound the ball makes as it passes through the hoop,
The way Manchester United win the FA nearly every year,
The way the new fabric of clothes feel against my skin,
The feel of my guinea pig's silky fur which rubs my skin.

I love these things.

Kayleigh Kirkman (12)
Hartford High School

MEMORIES OF MINE

I like the feeling of Fridays, knowing I am free,
The sound of music and rhythm pounding in my ears.
I love the tangy taste of strawberries slowly melting down in my mouth,
My best feeling is when a plane takes to the air and your stomach
is churning all around.
I can also remember the sad times, coming home to see my dog,
and then to find he had gone.
I could feel the sadness building up inside me and the tears
trickling down my face.
These will be my memories for life.

Kylie Nancollas (12)
Hartford High School

MEMORIES

The soft, relaxing feel of wet sand in my toes,
The succulent taste of peaches and cream on my tongue,
The fizz of American soda up my nose,
The mind-boggling games at the museum,
The heavy dampness of a denim jacket,
The hungry glint in my pet rat's eyes,
The high shrill of a flute,
These are the things which I will remember forever.

Emily Pargeter (11)
Hartford High School

MEMORIES

The salty, vinegary taste of chips from the chippy.
The crunchy, cheesy taste of freshly baked hot pizza from the Caspian.
The exciting feeling shooting up and down my body
When I go for an away rugby match.
The fizzy, bubbly feeling on your tongue when you drink Coke.
The spicy, hot taste of curry when you put it in your mouth.

Christopher Atherton (11)
Hartford High School

I LOVE

I love the feel of my rabbit's beautiful, soft, warm fur.
I love the sound of popcorn as it pops in the microwave.
I love chocolate fudge as it melts in my mouth.
I love strawberry ice-cream as it freezes my lips.
I love the rain as it tap, tap, taps on my window.
This is what I love.

Catriona Gilmour (11)
Hartford High School

MEMORIES

The gooey chocolate
melting and fading away
in my mouth.

The soft, light feel of
silk lying in
my palm.

The feel of my rabbit's
fluffy, velvety fur.

The fire of Lilt
trickling down
my throat.

The soothing sound
of the piano
ringing in my ear.

The sun beaming
on my back.

These are my memories.

Emma Houghton (11)
Hartford High School

BITTER STORM

The wind howled like a wild dog
The clouds let out a great roar
Instructing the rain to commence
And caved in causing day to become night.

Tucked up and cosy in our beds
Oblivious to the screaming storm,
Competing with the thought
Of a tranquil night.

A clap of thunder and a flash of light
The storm will not give in
Until it sees the trembling of the
Occupants and their uneasy faces.

Not cosy anymore but restless
The warmth of the fire cannot persuade
The atmosphere to change
As we wait for the storm to fulfil its need.

Jenny Atkinson (15)
Hartford High School

TREES 'N' BREEZE 'N' CATS

As the ripples stall on the river's surface
they start to turn to waves.
The trees start swaying in the air
and homes turn to caves.

The darkness of the lovely cave
and no one else about.
A branch swings swiftly through the air
and gives a bloody clout.

I wander down the misty path
with bushes overhead.
I've never seen a wood before
that seemed to look so dead.
Until, out something sped!

The thing sped out at breakneck speed
it struck an iron bar.
The cat sat up and hobbled back
then got hit by a speeding car.

Mark Stevenson (15)
Hartford High School

MEMORIES

I can remember happy times like . . .
The time I went to the beach and I felt the soft sand tickle my toes,
Or when we got a cat and I felt his wet, bumpy tongue,
Or the first time I opened a can of Coke and I felt the Coke fizz
                                                    in my face,
Or the time I ate chocolate and I felt the sloppy chocolate dribble
                                                    down my throat.

I can remember sad times like . . .
The time my silky, fluffy rabbit died,
Or the time I broke my arm and I had to wear an ugly, smelly
                                        plaster on my arm!
Or the time I cut my knee and I cried, the tears trickled down my face.

These are the memories I will never forget.

Sophie Milne (11)
Hartford High School

VICTIM

It's bubbling away quietly, showing no sign of explosion.
The red lava swirling and twisting as the pressure builds upwards.
It's shimmering violently, pain and pressure building.
Hours and days pass, any minute it's going to explode, any second now.
Finally it cracks, pain, pressure and tension all released
Into one huge mass of red lava, screams and tossing of smoke,
Letting it all out at once.
Hours later it settles and the simmer waits to overflow again.
This is what it is like to be bullied.

Lucy Lambert (13)
Hartford High School

THINGS I LOVE

The cool taste of ice-cream on a hot sunny day.
Drinking a warm mug of hot chocolate, watching my favourite soap.
The chewy taste of treacle toffee, from my favourite sweet shop.
I love going shopping for hours with my best friend.
Playing 'tig' in the park with my little brother, running around
                                                  and falling over.
The crunchy taste of hot pepperoni pizza with a freezing cup of Coke.
Listening to my favourite pop band with the volume right up.
The sight of a little puppy running and barking after the stick
                                        that their owner's just thrown.
Going to Cornwall, entering a joke competition with my parents
                                                  as the judges!
Half asleep, having a dream and waking up with the feeling
                    that I had just been thrown from Heaven into my bed.

These are the things that I love most.

Sarah Parkinson (11)
Hartford High School

MEMORIES

The moist feel of toffee fudge melting in my mouth
My fluffy mischievous rabbit scampering around my room
The soft feeling of sand in my toes.
The loud boom of my favourite record playing.
The swish and glide of my body rushing through the water.
The fizz and tingle of Coke sloshing down my throat.
Rushing down a water slide with the water spraying in my face.
The hot taste of pepperoni pizza sizzling in my mouth.

These are my memories.

Ceri Polglass (11)
Hartford High School

A Sky In Torment

I stand alone here now,
The breeze has stilled,
And although
Through the perfect reflection,
Of which the smooth surface of this mere emits,
The world seems at peace.

It is not,
The air hangs still around me,
Heavy around me,
Foretelling inevitable destruction,
The optimistic song of the dawn,
Silenced,
Killed,
As slowly unnatural darkness falls upon this earth,
Creeping in,
A slowly lumbering giant of the sky,
Beating back the sun.

All is dark is now,
The sun surrendered,
And now the wind rises,
The servant of the storm,
Hissing through the trees,
Now!

A piercing white light,
Illuminating this night within day,
Briefly linking earth with terrible sky,
Thunder rolls overhead,
This sky in torment,
The might of the storm now upon me.

Darkness,
Light and sound colliding in my mind,
Like an orchestra in disarray,
I run,
But seemingly never forward,
For my own insignificance is confirmed in the driving rain,
Which stings with hail,
The shrapnel of this war.

Sky and earth repel,
My feelings numbed with cold,
Soul,
Body,
Mind defeated,
This mere reflection shattered,
A world in chaos.

Chris Eves (15)
Hartford High School

THE MONSTER

T   iny, small legs and arms, with eyes on the end of its fingers and toes,
H   uge, great eyes wobbling when he walks,
E   normous teeth, dirty yellow dirt taking over them.

M   oths buzzing around its big, bulging head,
O   ne gooey eye, bright yellow with a tiny black pupil,
N   ails full of dirt, long and spindly, that twirl right out,
S   limy green with thousands of multicoloured scales,
T   reacherous mouth that only smiles when it likes,
E   xcess fat that hangs loosely on its tummy,
R   *uuuunnnnn!*

Lydia Woodman (12)
Hartford High School

COLD MORNING

The sun shines brightly, low in the sky.
The deceptive light outside gives a false impression of heat.
Once your eyes fall on the floor and you see the frost glistening,
The illusion is gone.
I step out of my warm haven and into the morning air.
The air is still and bitterly cold, but, for some reason it tastes pure.
The steam coming from my mouth as my breath meets the cold air,
Looks as if I have a fire inside.
The walk along the road is not easy.
I seem to slide everywhere on the ice-rink path.
When I reach my destination the doors seem to welcome me
As if saying 'Come in from the cold.'
I enter and leave the cold morning behind me.

Gareth Freeman (16)
Hartford High School

WHAT IS IT LIKE TO BE ME

B   ullied throughout the day
U   nhappy with what I say
D   epressed at home at night
D   ifferent when I have to fight
Y   ou call me names

C   owardly things they want me to believe
L   onely when she had to leave
A   ngry when I have to lie
R   ejected when I always try
K   nocked back down it is always the same.

Emma Howman (14)
Hartford High School

MEMORIES

My hand on my pet's soft fur.
My accomplishment of overcoming *oblivion*!
My bouncy, wouncy bed.
Completing all the rides at Water World.
When I won a 9 to 12 drawing competition.
When I bought my first packet of those annoying Pokémon cards.
When I stayed off school for brilliantly breaking my nose.

Callum Gibson (11)
Hartford High School

DON'T START

I'll destruct and corrupt you,
I am revolting and mischievous,
You'll become sinful and unhealthy,
Since I'm vile and poisonous.
As I am your shameful and rotten friend:
Do you ever want to know me?
As I am ghastly and rotten.

Rebecca Thirsk (15)
Hartford High School

WITCHES

W hen the darkness comes out they creep into the night.
I n tall dark hats and with their cats on their brooms.
T he witches gather as their coven meeting begins.
C ats settle down next to the bubbling cauldron.
H erbs and spices are thrown in to make a spell.
E very witch starts chanting, waving their hands in the air then
S pooky things start to happen.

Alex Clare (12)
Hartford High School

WINTER DAYS

I awake in my room
Seeing the snow slowly creep forward.
Crystallising everything in its wake,
The icicles hang down like bats of the night,
Waiting to glide out of their icy tombs.

Kids pull themselves through the snow,
Like a dying mammoth just trying to go that yard further
Than its fallen counterpart.
As I open the door the wind turns me grey with its shriek,
Winding, whistle, like the sound of the cars locking brakes
As they hit their fate.
A tree branch gives way to a strangling snow
Like an old man to an old ground-down heart,
This is truly winter days.

Thomas Beard (15)
Hartford High School

WITCHCRAFT

W itches now, witches then,
I n their caves, and in their dens,
T heir familiars sing and dance,
C ats and bats and even ants,
H erbs and spices in the pot,
C auldrons bubbling quite a lot.
R ising up the sun is awaking,
A way they go, the dawn is breaking,
F lying off each one alone
T ill next time, they fly back home.

Holly Evans (12)
Hartford High School

NATURAL VIOLENCE

Sitting alone in my dark cell
I watch the monster at work
The sky turns a sullen black
Bleaching the light away
A rumble of anger echoes from above
As electric blades tear open the ground
The trees bend their backs
Clearing the way
For the howling creature approaching
I look out from the window
Which defended my face
From the bullets that shot from the sky
They scratched and clawed at the glass
Wanting to shatter their way through
But instead, trickle down miserably, defeated
The horizon, an image of pain
Displays the ocean contorting in agony
Waves curl and crash against the sand
Shedding droplets of blood
Isolated, I listen to the house groan
As if the wind, an almighty hand
Has clasped the house and is squeezing
I sit back, thankful for my shelter
Hidden and protected
From the rage of natural violence.

Donna Kryger (15)
Hartford High School

THE BEACH

We pulled up in the car park of the beach, totally deserted
We walked over the wooden bridge that stood eight feet high
Dropping into the beach
The sand was so fine and soft
The sea was crystal clear, as blue as the sky

My brother and I sat there building sandcastles
While my sister and dad played in the sea
My mum lay there in the midday sun
Hoping for the tan she had always dreamed of

The tide started to come in
My brother and I frantically built up barriers to stop the water
Hitting our sandcastles we were fighting a hopeless battle
We were soon forced off the beach beaten back like a lion in a pen.

Joshua Dean (15)
Hartford High School

MATHS POEM

The bell rings, people slowly walk in,
Screwing up old homework and aiming for the bin,
The teacher walks in, we all stand up,
He says 'Sit down,' holding tea in a cup,
We open our books to the page we're at,
At the back of the room I am usually sat,
The first page I see is percentage, the second is graphs,
I bet you can guess this lesson is maths,
The lesson passes 5 minutes at a time,
Soon it will be dinner, I am ready to dine,
Now it's time for homework, oh what a mess!
I wish we had the lesson maths less and less.

Katie Garner (12)
Hartford High School

THE WITCH NEXT DOOR

There's an old witch next door,
Who collects frogs, dogs and more,
Her house is dark and dull,
And her pet familiar is a bull,
She cackles all day,
She cackles all night,
She practices magic with all her might,
Once she put a spell on me,
Which made me think I was a bee,
All day long I buzzed around,
Smirking, she watched, not making a sound.

There's an old witch next door,
Who collects frogs, dogs and more,
She's tall and thin,
With a hairy, pointy chin,
My mum said it's rude to stare
But I just can't help but glare!

Hayley West (12)
Hartford High School

MEMORIES

I can remember the funny times when I was smaller.
The chocolate that had melted in the sun all over my face
The fluffy sweet bunny jumping all over my bed
The deafening chants of the football fans making me cry
Clothes against my skin feels like silk
In Blackpool walking along the beach
The relaxing feel of sand between my toes
The drink of Sprite that's alright but Coke is better!

Christopher Moore (12)
Hartford High School

WITCHES

Hubble, bubble, toil and trouble,
Witches gathering in a coven,
Meet in a Shira once every two years,
With all the warlocks for good cheer,
Cackle, cackle, cackle,
All this noise aroused suspicion,
Of the local village, when,
Into town rode a witch hunter,
With his fellow warlock men,
Cackle, cackle, cackle,
The witches laugh and gamble,
The villagers are moving in,
Closing round the terrible din,
Warlocks scattered, witches caught,
The ones that were though really fought,
Cackle, cackle, cackle,
The witches were trailed and guilty found,
In front of the village's merry men,
Crackle,
The flames were burning,
Crackle,
The vicar said,
Crackle,
Lay rest these witches,
Crackle,
Dead!

Steven Quayle (12)
Hartford High School

THE WITCH

In the forest, there is a scream of a tormented soul,
As she comes across the thing everyone fears.
The witch.
She runs from that place but the hag's horrible
Cackling follows her all the way home.

In the forest's dark heart is a cottage, pond as black as night,
Door of deepest ebony. Here resides,
The witch.
Lamp-like eyes peer through the window and
Are gone as suddenly as they appeared.

Torches float towards the door,
Axes at the hands of townsfolk do their work,
Opening the grim portal to all those who dare enter.
The chant resounds throughout, *witch, witch, burn the witch!*
But alas, the evil crone has fled, leaving only a
Magic circle throbbing with used power . . .

Sam Chapman (12)
Hartford High School

ANIMALS

The lone wolf lets out a melancholy howl at the mysterious vast sky,
The scuttling mouse is timid and shy.
The beady eyes of the hunting hawk, search desperately for its prey,
The mighty and powerful lion, dreams idly throughout the day.
The monkey swings from tree to tree, high above the ground,
The spider spins its magical web, never making a sound.
The elegant, swift dolphins leap high above the waves,
The fierce and hostile bear, dwells deep inside its cave.

Jessica Hagerty (14)
Hartford High School

THE WITCHES' COVEN

W itches at the cold black coven
I n the dead of the night
T he cauldron froths and bubbles over
C ats run round with sheer delight
H owling and cackling comes to an end
E verything is quiet
S o off they go flying to and fro in the silver moonlight.

Lauren Truscott (12)
Hartford High School

WITCHES

W itches gather at a coven
I n a circle chanting spells,
T he familiars stay away near tall trees
C auldrons bubbling with magic brew
H erbs and spices thrown into it
E erie clothing to match their personalities,
S lithering snakes catch the scent of the potion.

Roy Doodson (12)
Hartford High School

IN TIMES FLOWN BY

In the times that have just flown by,
Women with a black cat or even a woman
That dealt with herbs
Would be tortured, their thumbs crushed,
Limbs put in leg vices, scorched
And punished in every way,
The world was a terrible place.

Matthew Petch (12)
Hartford High School

THE COVEN

W itches gather up at night round a fire with a cat
I n the cauldron are some herbs, chanting witches with black birds.
T he witches dancing all day and night.
C razy spells will soon ignite.
H isses and crackles, something has happened.
E verything has gone so dark.
S uddenly something has appeared, it's very faint and not so clear.

Serge Beynon (12)
Hartford High School

THE WITCHES' POEM

W itches dancing, chanting and cackling
I n the deep dark woods they go
T errible spells and mysterious rhymes
C ats prowl big, black and fat
H erbs, spices and stinking iris
E very tangled branch rustling in the moonlight
S piders watching steadily for their long awaited supper.

Andrea Rugen (12)
Hartford High School

WITCHES' BREW

W hen the moon comes out at night
I n the dark, witches gather.
T o the mysterious coven they fly
C hanting and singing, dancing and cackling.
H erbs torn and tossed into a bubbling cauldron.
E vil voices murmuring. The spell is cast!
S unrise appears and everyone is gone.

Amy Challenor (12)
Hartford High School

WITCHES

W omen all over are being accused of witchcraft for just being
   in the woods or having a black cat.

I t is appalling the amount of women and men getting killed
   for no reason.

T o stop this we will have to find a better way of checking if they
   are a witch or not.

C ats purr around all night, killing mice and chasing butterflies.

H erbs and spices boiling, the perfect spell of darkness
   and in some cases whiteness.

E choes scream around towns at night when the witches
   are about to hang.

S izzling toads, bouncing bats as the witches dance
   around the fire at the coven.

Stuart Jamieson (12)
Hartford High School

THE MONSTER THAT LIVES IN THE CELLAR

Its head is translucent,
changing colour from
blue to green.
Its arm-shaped blobs
extending from its stomach.

Everything it touches it can imitate:
first a tree, then a car.
If you ever see a moving house
or a tree that wasn't there before,
then that will be the monster,
the monster that lives in the cellar.

Christopher Popplestone (12)
Hartford High School

THROUGH THAT DOOR

Through that door,
I see spring
And there is no law,
That the buds can cover the floor.

Through that door,
I see summer,
The heat like a roar,
As it heats the earth to the core.

Through that door,
I see autumn
And I just want to soar,
Above it all forever more.

Through that door,
I see winter,
Snow covering the floor,
(It's a bit of a bore).

Suzanne Page (13)
Hartford High School

WITCHCRAFT

W omen were accused of witchcraft,
I f they had a cat, grew herbs or cooked in a pot,
T ortured terribly, thrown in rivers or burnt at the stake,
C hildren were also accused of witchcraft,
H orrendous treatment was given while they were paraded
through the streets,
E veryone came out to watch the terrible torture,
S o many innocent women were killed.

Emma Johnson (12)
Hartford High School

THE DEATH OF A WITCH

I see a witch hot and burning,
On the stake, her life twisting and turning,
Everyone calling her witch,
Wanting to toss her into a ditch,
Life is weird for an innocent in Hell,
When the last thing she hears is her cat's bell.

Another witch is dunked to drown,
Whilst everyone starts to frown,
Witches cackle with crooked noses,
Plants droop and dead are the roses,
She survives, she's a witch after all,
When the powers of good are beginning to fall.

Another two are to be hung,
And when they are dead they are to be slung,
Into a dungeon to be forgotten about,
To stop spreading diseases like palsy and gout,
One is alive, the other is dead,
She uses her powers, everyone's faces are red.

Alex Martin (12)
Hartford High School

WITCHCRAFT

W icked witches and wizards haunt the night.
I n the cauldron boils snakes' eyes and bats' blood.
T hrough the night they cackle and shriek.
C hanting together as they boil potions.
H earing the wolves howl in the distance.
E ach and every witch flying round on broomsticks.
S aying goodbye as night falls.

Kim O'Grady (12)
Hartford High School

THROUGH THAT DOOR

Through that door there is a castle,
His lordship is having a feast,
Servants run around causing hassle,
Taking food to the old priest.

Through that door there is a jungle
With monkeys that swing
And cubs curled up in bundles,
Then there's the lion, he's the king.

Through that door there's a land made of sweets,
There's a chocolate village, yum, yum
And a garden full of your favourite treats,
Enough to fill your tum.

Through that door there is an ocean,
It's calm on top
But underneath it's a world full of motion,
There's fish that dart and plants that flop.

Katie White (12)
Hartford High School

WITCHES AT NIGHT

W hen the night creeps in the witches call,
I   n the deep dark wood a coven forms,
T he witches chant to charm the poisonous contents of the cauldron,
C ats prowl and prance, guarding the witches' den,
    far in the bed of trees,
H erbs and holly berries bubble and boil,
E choes of ear piercing shrieks,
S hudder through the trees at the dead of night.

Frances Buckley (12)
Hartford High School

THROUGH THE DOOR

Through the door
To the Dominican Republic
The air is warm
The people swarm
We get to the terminal
To collect our bags
Then we get on a bus
And make a fuss
Through the door

Through the door
Onto a stage
Placebo play
I could dance all day
Here comes David Bowie
He signs my book
REM are playing now
They're so cool - wow
Through the door

Through the door
Is the Friends set
Chandler smiles at me
So does Ross and Joey
Monica cooks me food
Rachel shows me her clothes
Phoebe plays me a song
That I knew all along
Through the door

Through the door
Is boring old school
The teachers give you work
With a nasty smirk
The lessons are boring
The weather is cold
I've forgotten my food
Now I'm in a mood
Through the door.

Katy Wilson (12)
Hartford High School

THROUGH THAT DOOR

Through that door,
There is a football pitch,
Where all the crowd
Are cheering and booing.

Through that door,
There are children playing,
Shouting in a secret garden.

Through that door,
The sign of spring,
As trees are budding
And daffodils growing.

Through that door
A haunted house,
Creaking windows,
Scary ghosts,
Go in there if you *dare!*

Richard Cain (12)
Hartford High School

THROUGH THAT DOOR

Through that door
Is a magic land
As pretty as can be
With streamers, banners and a marching band
And a clear blue sea

Through that door
Is a swimming pool
Swimmers up and down
The water is not warm, but cool
And spectators all around

Through that door
Is a spooky room
In the roof a leak,
The door shuts behind me with a boom.
And the floorboards go creak, creak

Through that door
Is a snooker board
Green, yellow and black
Pot a ball and your losing turns are cured
And eventually you will get the knack.

Kathryn James (12)
Hartford High School

BIG GREEN MONSTER

Big green monster,
Ready for lunch,
Slither over the slimy sludge,
Gobble, gobble,
Crunch!

Under the murky water,
He licks his lips and sees
Ten big pink wriggling toes
Attached to a pair of knees!

Nathan Booth (12)
Hartford High School

THE BEAST

The trees shrank down,
intimidated by the natural power
fighting against them.
The wind pushes through,
showing no mercy
scared leaves turn away
in fear of the strength.
A flash illuminates the black canvas.

Alone, watching.

The intensity of black clouds
causes shadows to reign.
Brightness of the day annihilated.

Sitting, staring
the faint threatening growl of the beast,
waiting to pounce.

I watch and witness this phenomenon
as the growling creature rolls in,
it brings with it bolts of white,
and creeps up with an ominous roar.
It attacks and brings a new air of destruction.

Beth Anderson (15)
Hartford High School

THROUGH THAT DOOR

Through that door
A mystery world,
Where no one had
Ever been before.
A holly bush,
It shook with life
With flowers everywhere
In sight.

Through that door
A football pitch,
The fans all cheering me on.
I ran with all my life
And scored a goal
A hat-trick,
And one.

Through that door
The laundry lies,
It's spooky and slimy
There's nowhere to hide.
The clothes and towels
Are moving around,
I can't get out of here.

Martin Williams (12)
Hartford High School

BLACK

I'm black, and I am screaming inside,
it's like I am a show at a zoo.
I'm black and there's nowhere to hide,
I'm different, I'm scared and I'm lonely.

I'm black and I feel like lashing out,
why does everyone hate me, why not someone else?
I'm black, without a doubt,
is there really any meaning to my life?

Nicole Tooze (13)
Hartford High School

THROUGH THE DOOR

Through the door
A gloomy hall opened out,
Wooden floors and patterned carpets,
Curved staircase with wooden banisters,
Old grandfather clock ticking in the corner.

Through the door
A study was shown.
One leather-topped desk,
Piles of scattered paper,
Expensive books and old pens.

Through the door
A bright kitchen appears,
A strong cooking aroma greets me,
Saucepans full of bubbling rich food,
A table laid out.

Through the door
A beautiful garden transforms
Plenty of colourful flowers,
Green, lush grass,
Birds singing.

Stephen Shields (12)
Hartford High School

THROUGH THE DOOR

Through the door
is the rink,
I skate onto the ice
and hear the cheers of the fans,
and then let the game begin,
then those words, I've scored.

Through the door,
where am I?
Then 'Where's the gorilla?
Here you are.'
'No, no, no, you've got the wrong person.'
'Just get the suit on.'
Cameras, oh no! I'm on a film set.

Through the door
my dream team Liverpool.
'Hey kid, come train with us,'
'Who me?'
'Yes, you.'
I'm really at Liverpool's training ground,
oh no, I cannot play football.

Through the door
is the garden,
with the daffodils lining the
red brick wall.
Through the door
is the greenhouse
where the tomatoes climb the glass walls,
where are we?
My garden.

Kevin Tierney (12)
Hartford High School

MONSTER POEM

The monster was grey-green,
It looked like a blob,
It was everywhere you went.
One eye on his forehead,
No nose, no ears,
Just a small mouth,
Twenty fingers on one hand, three on the other.
Jumping out on you, pouncing,
Ready to eat you for his tea.
His lips were on his legs,
It gurgles, it splutters,
Then it disappears.
Nowhere to be seen,
Until tea time, it shows its face.
It's horrible: a slimy green, terrifying guarantuan face.

Rebecca Beech (12)
Hartford High School

ZUDOMON

Zudomon's Vulcan Hammer smashes Digimon into pieces,
His heavily armoured body is made of spikes and muscles,
He stomps slowly, but catches the Digimon, then quickly sends
                            a blow of victory at its head,
Zudomon's head has fangs for teeth and a jagged horn with spikes,
His eyes glint in the sun, setting a deadly glance,
He scrapes with his claws as big as talons,
He carries his master on his head and harms anyone else,
The way you find that Zudomon's been in town is the destruction
                            in his path.

Joseph Woodman (12)
Hartford High School

THROUGH THAT DOOR

Through that door,
I look and see,
A magical sea,
An upside down world,
Where between you and me,
Mermaids swim,
A water world,
Full of slides and fun things,
Never dull or boring,
I watch them swim,
And then something catches my eye,
A dolphin,
Blue as the sea goes by.
Through that door,
I look and see,
The lovely crisp sun,
On a warm summer's day.
Through that door,
Creeping, crawling, ready to pounce,
A splendid, spotted, soft coat,
Gleaming in the bright sun,
Graceful with powerful paws,
Shining teeth.

Jessica Woods (12)
Hartford High School

THROUGH THAT DOOR

Through that door
Is my own special place,
I can do anything
In my own special place,
I have a TV,
If I get bored, just in case.

Through that door
Is Anfield, Liverpool's ground,
The team kit is red,
Get paid every week £50,000
Home of The Kop,
Liverpool, my team that I found.

Through that door
Is a wrestling ring,
I'll be a wrestler,
I'll be called the 'Death King'
I'll win every match,
With a back breaker swing.

Through that door
Is a swimming pool
Full of water
To keep me cool.
I won't drown,
I won't be a fool.

Philip Atkinson (12)
Hartford High School

THROUGH THE DOOR

Through the door I can see,
Buffy and Angela,
fighting a demon but where can it be?

Through the door I can see
dolphins bobbing in front of the boat,
looking at the crystal clear sea.

Through the door I can see
a beautiful garden full of yellow and orange daffodils,
lots of animals especially the bee.

Through the door I can see
a massive bedroom with lovely colours,
a pretend beach and even a pretend sea,
or is it real?

Jesse Dean (12)
Hartford High School

WITCHES

Riding hoovers through the night,
Here come the witches with all their might.
Gradually getting nearer and nearer,
Every second getting weirder and weirder.
With green faces and pointed noses,
With cats with tails like garden hoses.
They've got black cloaks with hats to match,
Here come the witches with all their might.

David Bucknell (12)
Hartford High School

THROUGH THE DOOR

Through the door I walk
And what do I see,
Camera and film crews,
And the star, well it's me!

Through the door I wander,
But where am I now?
I'm walking on rainbows and clouds
But how?

Through the door I go
Now I'm on a boat
Sailing on a sea of dreams
Gently bobbing afloat.

Through the door I fly,
Giving a grumble or groan,
Where am I now?
Never mind, I'm home!

Naomi Hall (13)
Hartford High School

WITCH

W atching, waiting, the look of anger on their faces
I nside, I can feel my heart beating like crazy
T he executioner smiling, showing his yellow teeth
C hildren booing and hissing as he raises his arm
H earing voices shouting *kill, kill* in the distance
E ven my mind is saying I will never live
S uddenly with one swipe of a lever my life will end.

Carla Peters (12)
Hartford High School

THROUGH THAT DOOR

Through that door
Is a watery floor
Where the dolphins roam
And call it home.

Through that door
Are children screaming for more,
Springing around and around,
Looking at the ground.

Through that door
Where the people go 'cor'
Is a magic land
Where there is a bright big band.

Through that door
Is a tidy floor,
Teddy's on the bed
And on the pillow is a head.

Helen Wood (12)
Hartford High School

MONSTER!

M ouldy and slimy like an old piece of bread,
O ld and withered, ready for bed,
N o one had seen it, it was gooey and red,
S o what is this monster to be?
T atty and old, bolshie and bony,
E lectronic and buzzing, ready to eat,
R eally what is this thing?

Deryn Blythe (12)
Hartford High School

JOURNEY

We are all on a voyage into our very own minds.
Running back and forth into its depths.
Sometimes it seems that life is just a big joke
And we are all just punchlines.
Compensating one thing for another.
Shuffling our psyche, searching for nothing.
All you'll ever have to rely on is yourself.
Take away that and you're as good as dead.
We are all on a voyage into our very own souls.
Diving deep into its murky depths.
Sometimes it seems that life is just an enigma,
And we are all just another little puzzle.
Exchanging thoughts and feelings for something else.
Perplexing every one and everything.
All you'll ever have to rely on is yourself.
Take away that and you're as good as dead.
We are all on a journey into our very own hearts.
Plunging straight head first into its depths.
Sometimes it seems that life is just a hallucination,
And we are all just images in time.
Throwing away our views and opinions.
Becoming a neurotic and disturbed.
All you'll ever have to rely on is yourself.
Take away that and you're as good as dead.

David Wade (14)
Hartford High School

DARKNESS

I lie alone in bed, it's dark,
　　I look around the room,
The shadows look like different shapes
　　In the light of the moon,
My clock upon the wall ticks loud,
　　It looks just like a face,
The dull and dreary curtains flap
　　All over the dark, dark place,
The darkness sometimes makes me think
　　Of monsters under my bed,
They creep and crawl, some tall, some small,
　　That's what my brother said,
I lie alone in bed, it's dark,
　　I look around the room,
Until I fall asleep which is quite soon!

Sarah O'Connor (11)
Hartford High School

WITCH POEM!

W　hen the sun's gone down, the moon rises.
I　n the sky the witches fly.
T　o the coven the witches go.
C　ats as familiars following behind.
H　erbs and spices the witches gather.
E　very familiar sat behind the witches.
S　o the night goes on, the witches go back, the night's gone down,
　　the sky's not black.

Gareth Evans (11)
Hartford High School

CRUELTY

What? No!
It can't happen!
Those women could be innocent.
Children depend on their mother.
How would you like it if your mother was
Either burnt or drowned? If you
Spy on them or suspect them of witchcraft, they could soon be dead!

Philip Procter (12)
Hartford High School

IT'S NOT FAIR

Why's it me that always gets picked on?
Just because,
I don't wear trousers and always wear jeans.
I always have a carrier bag and not a normal bag.
In my jumper there is a hole, it is very small too.
I get called names just because I am not normal,
And even the teachers pick on me.

Samantha Cain (13)
Hartford High School

MATHS

Maths is good, maths is great
My favourite number is eight
I know my 2s, I know my 4s,
I know that 12 x 12 is 144.

Leon Hewitt (12)
Hartford High School

THROUGH THAT DOOR

Through that door
I see peace
Not war!
I see friendship
Not fighting!
I see playing fields
Not minefields!
The only weapons I see
Are the ones I eat with!
And I see a door.

Through that door
I see future
Not present!
I see people living on the moon
Not Earth!
I see hover cars
Not ones with wheels
I see us going to Mars for our holidays
Not Paris or Spain!
I see robots doing the house chores
Not our mums or house cleaner!
I see DVD on our home cinema screen
Not a VCR on a twenty-eight inch TV!
And I see a door.

Through that door
I see past
Not present!
I see Vikings
Not the Royal Navy!
I see catapults
Not Lancaster Bombers!

I see Romans marching
Not the armies travelling by tanks!
I see them fighting with swords
Not shooting people with guns!
And I see a door

And through that door is home.

Steven Goodwin (13)
Hartford High School

THE SEASIDE

Driving to the seaside
The first thing I notice
Is the smell of the sea,
The smell of salty water
Tells me that we are near the beach.

As we walk along the prom
The sweet smell of candyfloss
Reaches my nostrils,
I feel that I could float
On its pink cloud.

After a day of fun on the fair
You start to get hungry
And the delicious aroma
From the fish and chip shops
Draws you in.

The fresh smell of the outdoors
Refreshes you and calms you down
When you are tired,
But it can also lead you
To a fun day ahead!

Kim Donal (12)
Hartford High School

MONSTER!

Horns like a bull,
Jaw of a lion,
Head of a hammerwhale,
Eyes of a frog,
Longer claws than a cat,
Tail like a horse,
Legs like cheetahs,
Nose similar to a dog,
You may think you'd need a qualification,
But it is floccinaucinihilipilification!

Michael Lawrence (12)
Hartford High School

THE . . .

Size big or small
In fact any size at all

Extremely fat or extremely thin
Depends what mood it's in
Bad face or big grin
Good mood or committed a sin?

Can change into any creature
Shape or size
It's always a big surprise.

Peter Blain (12)
Hartford High School

THE JELLY MONSTER

Jennifer the jelly monster
Wobbling all around.
She lives in the sea
Where she can't be found.

Jennifer the jelly monster
Longing for a hug.
With her slimy tentacles
Don't take her for a mug.

Jennifer the jelly monster
Is quite an *ugly* thing.
Though shy she is
She can really sting!

Jennifer the jelly monster . . .
Well what else can I say?
She's jellier than jelly
Quite a price to pay!

Sarah Brookes (12)
Hartford High School

THE CREEPER

There's a slimy, slithery thing,
It's underneath my bed, and it's lurking.
It's creepy and crawly, it's totally yuck,
The thing leaves big footprints and a lot of muck.
It's making funny noises underneath my bed,
Its scaly, slithery, silver head
Looks like it's dead
But it scares me!

Emma Davies (12)
Hartford High School

DO YOU KNOW HOW IT FEELS?

Do you know how it feels to be
Mocked
Isolated?
I do.
Do you know how it feels to be
Guilty
Empty
And lonely?
I do.
Do you know how it feels to be frustrated?
Do you ever think about running away and wishing
There was a land just for you,
Where everybody would just take you for who you are?
I do.

Kayley Hughes (13)
Hartford High School

MATHEMATICS

M ultiplication mayhem
A nswers I would like
T ables I find difficult
H ow can I get them right?
E mpty is my head now
M y mind has gone blank
A nd the teacher wants an answer
T ut, him I cannot thank
I 'm just no good at tables
C alculator's what I need
S till, I'm good at English (it's easy to write and to read!)

Steven Smith (12)
Hartford High School

WHY IS IT ALWAYS ME?

People pick on me
because I'm not cool.
Why is it always me?

> People laugh at me
> they think I'm a fool.
> Why is it always me?

> > People sneer at me
> > because I don't look right.
> > Why is it always me?

> > People hate me
> > I cry every night.
> > Why is it always me?

> People look at me
> because I don't fit in.
> Why is it always me?

> > How come it's never them?
> > Why is it always me?

Katy Tomlin (13)
Hartford High School

FEELINGS

Every day I dread waking up
to another day of pain.
It's not just children
it's teachers too that show their racist ways.
Do you know how this feels?
How this feels deep, deep, deep inside?

Stacey Christie (14)
Hartford High School

CONSCIENCE

Tut, maths again,
That boring old teacher,
algebra AKA gibberish,
What are we doing today?
Finish the chapters 1+2,
1+2 how can I finish them in this lesson?
I'm not blooming Superboy.
Quick, she's looking, best act like I'm working,
Doo de doo, da da dee
No, no, get on with your work Tom, c'mon,
Right x+y = . . .
Finished Miss,
Hey, finished already? Goodie, goodie,
Oops! Eh, did I say that out loud?

Tom Steggel (12)
Hartford High School

UNFORGETTABLE MATHS

It was dark and cold, I was not in a safe *area.*
I heard the door creak, someone was in close *range.*
The door *increased* its speed.
I saw someone from a *length.*
He or she was trying to *sum* me up.
Can you see him?
'Negative' said a voice.
I *estimated* that there was two of them.
'That's *odd*' I said 'I recognise that voice.'
I started to *add* my fear.
Boo! It was my brothers.
I *excluded* them out of my room.

Jamie Fleet (11)
Hartford High School

MEMORIES

The scrumptious taste of chocolate melting in my mouth.
The crack of a can of Coca-Cola being opened.
The fizzy lemon flavour of a sweet tingling my tongue.
The soft feel of a clean, new fleece on my back, warm and snug.
The irresistible smell of freshly baked bread.
The colours of a rainbow, a peacock showing off.

The sensitive, pink nose and the silky, sable fur of Misty, my hamster.
Going on holiday, meeting different people,
Foreign money, a strange new language.
The feel of soft golden sand under my feet.
The way the sun rises on an early school morning
Melting the dew on the daisies in the grass.

Neil Jacob (12)
Hartford High School

MUM

A flower in the garden, the one that stands out,
The leader, the wise one that's my mum, there's no doubt.
An evergreen in winter, a daffodil in spring,
A face in the darkness, or a huge diamond ring.
The shield from hatred, the cover from rain,
The warmth in the fire, the blockage from pain.
The yellow in the sun and the blue in the sky,
The birds when they sing and fly so high.
She's the sweetness in chocolate and softness in silk,
She's the flame on the candle and the whiteness in milk.
I will love her always, like I love the sunrise,
Tears roll down her cheek, how I hate it when she cries.

Helen Walker (14)
Hartford High School

MURDEROUS MATHS

Pie charts going dizzily round,
Bar charts shooting up then slowly coming down.
Confusing quadrants and decimal dilemmas
Are really dimming my mind.
Algebra arsonist is not what I'm famous for,
But formulas I can find.
Positive people or negative nerds,
Don't copy me or I'll tell.
1, 2, 3, 4, kill me with more.
Multiplication is mind-boggling,
Subtracting is sore,
Dividing is dim
And much, much more.
Nerves at my knees won't hold me up,
Test today and I haven't done my revision,
I'd better hurry up.

Elizabeth Newton (12)
Hartford High School

+ MATHS POEM -

D   ivision, symmetry and geometric shapes.
I   ncreasing homework filling a positive page.
V   ertices rotating across a multiplying perimeter
I   ncredibly irritating problems.
S   ymmetry rotating on squared paper.
I   deas clouding up a negative head
O   ncoming factors and prime numbers close by.
N   egative numbers, positive primes *homework noooooo . . .*

Lauren Davies (11)
Hartford High School

MATHS

Maths lessons, learning's fun
Come on, this sum must be done
As the time goes ticking by
My brain won't work, I wonder why?
It's this hard work I suppose
Next it's homework, here it goes.
Plus, minus, multiply, divide,
It's all going dim in my mind.
Square roots and shapes
4L - I don't know what it makes
Tests next *nooo*
Here we go
Got to revise
Oh what a surprise
Sometimes I pass
And sometimes I don't. Maths oh!

Sarah Yould (12)
Hartford High School

MONSTER POEM

I had a visitor one dark night
He came in my room to give me a fright.
He thundered along with his great big feet,
The wickedest monster you ever could meet.
He stared at me with his three beady eyes
And gave me an unexpected surprise.
I tried to scream but couldn't begin
When he smiled at me an enormous grin.
Now we're good mates my visitor and me
The friendliest monster there ever could be!

Lois Norman (11)
Hartford High School

THE COW

As it stands there big and bold,
It never seems to mind the cold.
Black and white, cream or brown,
It stands there all day with its head down.
Most times it stands, but sometimes lies,
Letting out strange loud cries.
It is curious and very nosy,
But its leather coat keeps it cosy.

As it wanders out of the field gate,
The rest of the herd realise it's too late.
It wandered onto the railway track,
Never even considering to look back.
The track all of a sudden began to shake,
To the cow it felt like a giant earthquake.
Round the corner the train did fly,
It hit the cow and tossed it into the sky.
The cow crashed down with a smack,
Unfortunately the cow had broke its back.

Peter Naylor (14)
Hartford High School

THINGS I LOVE DOING MOST OF ALL!

Going to America and Disneyland for the first time
The taste of white choc-chip ice-cream
Melting chocolate in my mouth
Getting my first pet and seeing the first baby guinea pig
The taste of my mum's chocolate cake
Listening to my favourite music
Talking to my friends
These are the things I love doing most of all.

Victoria-Jade Tidbury (12)
Hartford High School

SHADOWS

Shadows, shadows on the wall,
Creep and crawl across the floor.
Jumping up and swaying low,
Fall to create a scaring glow.
Moving from the depths of light,
To give me a dreadful fright.
Fearless of the moving night
It'll disappear when I turn on the light.

Davelee Brocklehurst (14)
Hartford High School

MATHS

M is for minus and multiply
A is for algebra - X plus Y
T is for times tables - seven times eight
H is for homework, you must not bring it late
S is for sums, so many to do,
    You will use maths your whole life through.

Helen Fuller (13)
Hartford High School

WRITER'S BLOCK

I'm having one of those days
Everything's going wrong in so many ways
I've got writer's block
Words are running amok
And I can't think how to end this poem.

Annie Stewart (14)
Hartford High School

THE WHIRLING WIND

Like a supernatural being,
He can't be seen but his presence is felt.
He sweeps the ground with a brush,
Whisking autumn leaves into the air.
Only to let them fall like confetti.
His breath forces the obedient trees to bow down before him.
His deafening roar silences all other sounds.
He grasps at debris and flings it to the ground in rage.
Then he spins like a pirouetting ballerina.
Turning faster than a spinning top,
Like an angry bull he tears up earth,
Caring for no one.
Nothing in his path is safe.
Destruction is inevitable.

Jack Lightfoot (15)
Hartford High School

GROWING UP

I really don't want to grow up
Develop a liking to coffee, all day I must sup.
No more school will be a bonus
But no more money our parents will loan us.
Getting away with things won't be so easy
Thinking of growing up makes me tremendously queasy.
Having to work all those hours a week
Or the opposite dead end jobs constantly I seek.
Either way I know I'll always be
Forever a kid at heart, that's me!

Eileen Greenwood (14)
Hartford High School

MOBILE PHONE FREAK!

All I want is a mobile phone,
It's not too much to ask.

All my friends, well they've got one,
So I'm all on my own.
If I want to send a text,
I have to use my dad's,
Now that just can't be fair,
So it's surely for the best!

All I want is a mobile phone,
It's not too much to ask.

Emma Walker (14)
Hartford High School

MATHEMATICS

M aths
A re a doddle
T imes tables
H omework
E quilateral
M easuring
A nd . . .
T ime
I nk pens
C urrency
S hapes.

Siobhan Eyes (12)
Hartford High School

ME AND YOU

Our mirrored eyes,
And mirrored nose,
Our identical hands,
And identical clothes.

We're the same height,
And the same weight,
We look the same,
Don't we mate?

I've known you all your life,
And you have mine.
We scream and shout,
At the same time.

We've been together,
Through thick and thin,
In fact you've been every place,
I've ever been.

I see you in the morning,
When I comb my hair,
You're my mirror-image,
You're always standing there.

Olive Hynes (15)
Hartford High School

THE SCARECROW

Unlike everyone else, I'm only two bones,
A broken broom handle and an old piece of cane.
My ragged gloves are holey and torn.
I wear the farmer's old clothes.
My coat and shirt are both undone,
My trousers are ripped and are coming unstitched.
My old hat is full of hay,
My only foot is stuck in the ground.
I stand up tall on top of a hill,
I stay there always,
Night or day,
Rain, snow or sun.
I wish the birds would come and nest in me,
I wonder why they always fly away.

Sarah Hallam (13)
Heath Comprehensive School

BAD POEM

May I have your attention please
It's the return of the unreal
Got a couple of screws in my head loose
You can't even stomach me
Let alone stand me
I'll be working at Burger King
Trying to get back my sovereign ring
This poem should be a head trip to listen to
Because I hate 90% of you
Sick of all you little boy and girl groups
Making my life a walking, talking, living hell
But who cares, it's just a bad poem isn't it.

Lee Hartigan (12)
Heath Comprehensive School

WWF ATTITUDE

The WWF has lots of superstars,
And they're all different shapes and sizes,
The only thing that you don't want is when the Big Show's hand rises.
Why not check into the Smackdown Hotel or visit the Undertaker
in Hell.

With a rush of flames,
Here comes Kane,
But then again,
There's Stephanie and The Game.
There's the death-defying
Moves of the Hardy Boyz,
Then across to X-Pac to make some noise!
But,
A special thanks to all the WWF and its superstars,
For without their tremendous talent,
This poem would not have been written.

Mike Delaney (12)
Heath Comprehensive School

SOUND

I can hear it, it's all around,
It's clear to my ears, that beautiful sound,
I can hear it vibrate and vibrate,
That catchy rhythm is impossible to hate,
Oh, listen to that delightful tune,
It can even be heard on the moon,
As it echoes in my ears,
It takes away all my fears,
Listen to the music!

Sarah Perraton (12)
Heath Comprehensive School

THE MAGICAL BONBON EXPERIENCE

It looks like a lumpy egg or a spherical dusty desert,
the dusty surface looks similar to the mountainous face of the Earth.

It smells like a tropical fruit bowl
with the wonderful scented aroma of strawberries.

It feels like a small pebble in need of smoothening.

It tastes like paradise, the sweetness of the bonbon urges you on
and creates a Caribbean atmosphere in your mouth.

When the bonbon has absorbed lots of saliva, it turns pink and softens
it is very difficult to resist this magnificent sensation.

After the bonbon has been devoured it leaves behind with it
a trace of a beautiful strawberry taste.

This taste carries you into an artificial sense of utter pleasure,
and brainwashes you so you carry on this Caribbean sensation
with an abundance of bonbons.

Harry Mills (12)
Heath Comprehensive School

THE OLYMPICS

O ver the handles, over the vault
L onger, higher, further, quicker than ever before.
Y achting got us two gold medals.
M en and women jumping, rowing and swimming for gold
P roving that Great Britain are the best.
I n hockey Britain were beaten.
C ould Britain get as many gold medals at the next Olympics?
S ydney was this year's Olympics, Athens is the next in
    four years time.

Thomas McNamara (12)
Heath Comprehensive School

ONE PLACE

Different than any other
Stranger than anything
Exploding with excitement
One place

Watching over it
A kind old owl
Waiting for intruders in
One place

There are different things there
Things never seen before
Living knights in shining armour
Giant owls staring at you
One place

But where are we?
Where could we be?
What is this one place
We have just seen?

Hayley Garnett (11)
Heath Comprehensive School

CHRISTMAS

Christmas is coming
The big cats are getting fat
The government is laughing
Cos they get all the VAT

The turkeys are escaping
Cos they don't want to die
They want you to go veggie
And eat some apple pie

The Christmas dinner's burning
The pudding has gone flat
My dad's drunk all the brandy
And now he is on his back

And now the season's over
The bills are coming in
My grandma said she's had enough
And is taking to the gin.

Gary Davies (15)
Heath Comprehensive School

CURSE

The sparks are all flying
In Henry Ford's workshop,
The fantastic new vibrating machines
Can't afford to stop.

Soon the cars will be polluting the air,
Which will destroy the ozone,
They should be making cars which run on air,
Because petrol will soon be forever postponed.

The humans are all bored now,
There's nothing to do in there,
All that they can do is
Watch and stare.

The mechanics are popular now,
There's breakdowns every day,
If this keeps carrying on,
They'll enjoy their pay day.

Paul Gavin (12)
Heath Comprehensive School

CHRISTMAS POEM

Christmas is coming
The children are all asleep
The Christmas stockings are hanging
On the chimney breast beneath

Santa Claus is coming
He will be here in a short while
To fill the stockings
With the toys what will make them smile

Jingle jangle went the sleigh bells
Bumping and banging down the chimney Santa came
He was dressed all in fur
From his head to his foot
And his clothes were all tarnished
With ashes and soot

He filled all the stockings
With such great stuff
Then he put his fingers
Aside of his nose
And giving a nod
Up the chimney he rose.

Gary Inett (15)
Heath Comprehensive School

THE POEM

Poems are for people with time to spare.
Poems are for people with time to care.
Poems can tell of joy and sadness,
Can bring feelings of happy times and gladness
And lights up the flame in my heart.

Poems tell a story.
Poems of faith and glory.
Poems can tell of my short life,
The memories flash like the edge of a knife.
My whole life, my poem.

Charlotte Johnson (12)
Heath Comprehensive School

TIGER

Lazy tiger in the sun,
Waiting for the moment.
Getting up he makes a roar,
Frightening its surroundings.
Walking down into the long grass
Of the African plains.

Prancing along, here comes his prey,
About to be chased for life or death.
Down the tiger crouches, waiting to pounce,
Creeping forwards as quiet as a mouse.

Nearer now his prey has come,
Getting up he shows his teeth,
Staring at it with his evil look,
Now's the time for him to make his move.

Up he comes with his ears high,
Racing faster than ever before,
He jumps up on his back and bites in hard.
Down his prey falls like a bag of rocks,
Dead on the ground.

He walks away feeling proud and full.

Nathan Davies (11)
Heath Comprehensive School

DESTRUCTION

Destruction, destroying and poverty,
Killing the world in its glory.
Polluting the world is not good,
We all should do as we should.
Many people die,
And go up in the sky.
All because of destruction,
       Destruction, destruction, destruction!

The world would be better,
If we wrote a letter,
Complaining about all the fuel
And how it is very, very cruel,
And tell that it's causing
       Destruction, destruction, destruction!

Adam Jones (11)
Heath Comprehensive School

LOST

Lost are things that cannot be seen,
Like a button behind a cupboard,
Old pennies inside an old couch,
Burnt, decaying rubber bands,
Old necklaces in a drawer, crying for freedom, all is lost.

Broken pencils are lost, when you no longer see them,
Ripped out pages that nobody can find,
Old shoelaces and little things,
That nobody ever notices,
They, in their own little world,
Want to be found.

Samantha Hawkins (11)
Heath Comprehensive School

THE ICE

Not a word came from him.
His skin pale,
His hair frozen.
His hope was fading.
Struggling to get higher and higher.

The sun suffocated the clouds,
The shivering ice
Makes him jolt.
Endless mountains of cold white ice.
His hope was fading.

The claws of his axe broke the ice.
Crumbling snow tickled his nose.
His hope was fading.
Suddenly he saw the top.
He won back his pride.

Sarah-Jane Getty (11)
Heath Comprehensive School

THE KNIGHT'S TOMB

The large brown owl swoops down to greet the knight's shining tomb.
The black cat is looking up, as the moonlight fills the room.
The sharp dagger standing on its point, as the statues stand
                                                    still and quiet.
The stained glass windows.
The gallant knight's sword.
The King's Holy Grail.
The chess-like floor, with the knights marching by.
As the water drops onto the picture, it vanishes!
Was it a reflection of my imagination?

Sophie Allan (11)
Heath Comprehensive School

GUINEA PIGS

Guinea pigs are small and round,
They also make a squeaky sound,
They run around, get in a muddle,
Then at night they like to cuddle,
They go to sleep in a pile of hay,
Then they come out the very next day,
Guinea pigs love to eat,
They run around on their tiny feet,
Guinea pigs can get quite fat
And sometimes get chased by a cat,
They sleep in hay
And eat all day,
Guinea pigs aren't very clever,
But they make the best pets ever.

Natalie Fletcher (11)
Heath Comprehensive School

THE CAT OF THE HELLMOUTH

The flame burned its magical inferno
As the nightmare claws transpire out from paw to toe
It came down from its radiant fireball
The eyes stared at nothing at all

When symbols show signs of warning
That this poor girl would not see the picturesque dawning
As this diabolical fiend dived for the catch
It killed and ripped her to attack

This machiavellian pussy to an evil girl
They disappeared with a twist and a whirl.

Jessica Agnew (11)
Heath Comprehensive School

SPIDERS

The spider is disliked by many people,
Spins a web in a holy church steeple.
With eight fine hairy legs of guilt,
Will spin a web as soft as silk.
The sunlight shows through a gap,
Till God turns on the enormous tap.
Spider's web is fully wet,
Unless the spider's kept a pet.
Fed with fat and juicy cricket,
Alive or dead he's not a picket.
He doesn't care where's his home
Even if it's on a telephone.
Until along comes a big shoe,
Which kills him and his memories too.

Leanne Wike (11)
Heath Comprehensive School

RED

Red is:
An eruption of molten lava,
A crystal ruby on an emerald stem,
A curing river of blood,
The breath of evil,
The raging bull's eye,
The horn on the Devil's head,
A beating heart,
A sinuous sea of wine,
The love of a beautiful woman,
The sign of danger.

Scott Swales (12)
Heath Comprehensive School

WINTER

I wake up and find our back garden
Encrusted with silver gems.
I rush outside and play around
This soft silver sparkling silk.
The old brown trees are iced like a cake
With white frosty frozen flakes.

The sun peeps out from behind the clouds
And slowly it starts to melt.
Soon I'm left with a cold Arctic slush.
Puddles are turning to ice.
In our pond is a small flat iceberg
And that is all we have left.

Michaela Rowlinson (11)
Heath Comprehensive School

HAMSTERS

Hamsters are tiny little creatures,
Tiny little creatures with extremely funny features,
In the day they curl up tight and sleep
Then in the night they come awake.

They scurry, scatter and even scratch
And sometimes they are hard to catch,
Once they're caught they like to cuddle,
Some time soon they'll get in a muddle.

Hamsters really like to eat,
Sometimes while they're half asleep,
But then again at the end of the day,
They go to sleep until their very next play.

Danielle Duncalf (12)
Heath Comprehensive School

PREDATOR

Predator of the green bushes,
Hidden deep away,
Until one small life passes,
Hoping to see another day,
He then raises his paws,
Out come diamond claws,
Which are as bright
As yellow flashing light,
He focuses his burning bright eye,
On the life passing him by,
Then one big roar,
Like hell broke out,
Hear the creature whimper and shout,
As snarling teeth dig deeper than deep,
Silky fur not asleep,
Then back into the green bushes,
And hidden deep away,
Until another life passes him,
Another day!

Alissa Tyrer (11)
Heath Comprehensive School

TRAPPED IN MAGIC

She was trapped in magic forever,
Fighting against the spell but never
Escaping from the mystery.
Swirling around in space,
Never changing the race
To break the fantasy.

Lois Browne (11)
Heath Comprehensive School

LFC

LFC is such a team
LFC is a boy's finest dream
Robbie Fowler with the cross to Owen,
The ball strikes the net and they're still going.

If they're 1-0 down they don't give up,
They act like a team and they're soon 2-1 up.

LFC are friendly and they play fair,
If they foul they don't argue
And they don't really care.

At the end of the match they make friends
With the other team.

I want to play for Liverpool,
That's my dream.

Andrew Nelson (12)
Heath Comprehensive School

It's Hallowe'en

It's Hallowe'en, hip, hip, hooray.
The ghosts and ghouls come out to play.

They'll eat you alive in the dead of night,
(I'm frightfully sorry if I gave you a fright!)

So don't despair if all's not well,
I'm going to give you a helpful spell.

'By hocus, by pocus, I wish you well,
May all ghoulies and ghosties say farewell!'

Beth Birmingham (15)
Heath Comprehensive School

THE LIVING?

Among the shadows of the yard,
There stands a mystical, creepy guard.
With his arms folded and his head up high,
He feels he could touch the cloudy sky.
The light draws near, his time has come,
Say hello to the blazing hot sun.
It's near dawn, what will he do?
He will soon disappear to see who?
The commander of the humid place Hell!
Which they name the great one Drell!
Or the gracious place where we all call Heaven,
Surrounded by his daughters, a total of seven.
And now the light has come again,
He has faded into nothingness in sorrow and pain!

Dawn Milliken (11)
Heath Comprehensive School

LIGHTNING

If I strike you alive, then you'll surely not survive,
Because I'm the king of the sky.
With my mate thunder we're kings of the night,
With a clash and a bang like we're having a fight,
Because I'm the king of the night.
I can kill, and so I will,
I'm jagged and tough, and surprisingly rough,
Because I'm the king of the sky.
I wouldn't hesitate, or death will be your fate,
I'm surely not dull, but I'm very harmful,
Because I'm the king of the night.

Michael Faragher (11)
Heath Comprehensive School

LEAP OF A DOLPHIN

The still water,
The sea breeze,
Calmly pushing back and back the seagulls,
Aqua blue,
A purple pearl,
Brightly shining green,
Mixes with the waves of the sea,
In and out, in and out,
The sea washes the shore,
The colour like a marble,
Swirling around the world,
Then suddenly with a splash,
A dolphin leaps,
Its back curved like a rainbow,
The sea sways,
With another splash,
The dolphin goes deep,
Into the mysterious sea,
The sea is calm again.

Laura Kinsley (11)
Heath Comprehensive School

COUNTRY SCENE

The water is flowing,
The stones are sill,
The blackness is growing,
As the clouds move at will.

The shadows are going,
The water is calm,
But the stones are staying,
As the sky has no harm.

The clouds are red,
The shadows are black,
The stones are nothing like a bed,
But the water never runs back.

Adam Glover (11)
Heath Comprehensive School

TOGETHER AT LAST
(Mutual feelings)

For so many nights I lay on my bed,
I wanted to die, I wished to be dead,
I'd never felt that pain before it cut me up inside,
I felt my heart was torn apart, I needed to decide,
Whether to live or whether to die,
Would my heart break, or would my heart fly.
My mind said forget it, but my heart would say no,
I needed to find you, I needed to know.
Would we have a future, or would I be alone?
Whatever way my life would go, I knew that I would have to know
If you loved me, if you cared,
I called you that day but now I am scared.
So now that I have got you here I'll never let you go,
I need you here to hold me close, I need for you to know
The way I feel inside for you grows stronger every day,
I need you here to hold me close, I need to hear you say,
You feel the same inside for me, you feel our love grow strong,
I want your body, I need your soul, my long lost love
I found once more, I love you, you're my soulmate,
You're my perfect kind of man,
I want to be forever yours to love and hold until the end.

Michelle Dwerryhouse (15)
Heath Comprehensive School

UNTITLED

They say the eyes are the windows of the soul,
My eyes are black, I cannot reveal myself,
Imprints remain of past people
Yet all I am left with is memories.

Soon to be solitary,
A black image that stands beside me is slowly edging away,
For Gaul is just beyond the blue mist,
Yet emotionally, it is a million miles away.

Bonheur Enfin - does this really exist?
Without the peacefully positioned arms of the tree around me, I am not sure.

The same sky covers us, the same sun beats down on us,
But it doesn't, I am here, they are there, my friend is there.
Days go by, years go by, lifetimes go by,
This monotonous repetition grows tiresome for no one but me.

These adolescent memories are packed into a shoe box,
Only to be recovered some 20 years on.
The pain, the death, the land comes flooding back.

Goodbye, adios, au revoir, language upon language
Nothing but communication separates us.

The familiar blackness is now just a speck in the distance,
Yet it is still the main image in my mind,
When I'm awake, when I'm asleep, every time I breathe it's on my mind.
I whisper my final words 'Au revoir, goodbye'
It all means the same thing,
Then close my eyes to a deep sleep.

Zoey Robb (15)
Heath Comprehensive School

DEATH ON THE STREETS

I'm not part of your group, I'm one of a kind,
I exist in your feelings, emotion and mind,
But you tried to block me out, say that I wasn't there,
That's why I hate you, why I don't really care.
But one thing's for certain, there won't be a next breath,
Because now, my friend your life has turned to death!

I'd follow you round, through your everyday life,
And being so different, I stuck out like a knife . . .
By day I would find you, wherever you were,
I never gave in, no matter how far.
Yes, by day I did hunting, worked on my own,
By night I did sleeping, chilled . . . to the bone.

Why do I do it, why don't I mourn?
I exist as this person for my heart has been torn.
Ha! I didn't deserve it anymore than you did.
Of course, you felt it literally; who am I trying to kid!
Once the rigor mortis sets in, we'll look quite alike,
Eternal brothers, from the family of spite . . .

We're both homeless now, but I did have one once . . .
A family and kids like some great ponce,
A business or two, and workers galore,
And all this I swapped, for us and nothing more . . .
But nothing will dissuade me, nothing will dilute,
I want to execute, I want to execute . . .

Kevin Stoba (13)
Heath Comprehensive School

THE SEA

I look out at the top of a cliff,
Down at a great blue ocean,
What great smell that I sniff,
Dawn at a great blue ocean,
The sun is about to set,
Down at a great blue ocean,
The great colours which project,
Down at a great blue ocean,
Gold, yellow, orange and red I see,
Down at a great blue ocean,
I wish I could take it home with me,
That great blue ocean.

Andrew Wike (13)
Heath Comprehensive School

I SEE A VISION

I see a vision,
It's television.
It brings joy,
Like a child with a new toy.
We watch it all day long,
We even sing along to the songs.
As we watch it day and night,
It may give some of us a little fright.
The only time I move away,
Is when someone has something to say.
I see a vision,
It's television.

Rebecca Jayne Hough (13)
Heath Comprehensive School

TELEVISION

Television is where you ought to be
Eat your supper and drink your tea.
You could come around, watch television with me.

It relaxes your body
Puts thoughts in your head
It's the television's fault if the hypnotism makes my brain go dead.
Go and tell your friends what the television has said.

I watch the television, it's so great
To watch the television is never too late.

You stare and glare until
Your eyes go square.

The only escape from the television's eye
Is to watch the little dot fade, then die.

Emma Callan (13)
Heath Comprehensive School

TELEVISION

Channel 1, 2, 3, 4
But if you have got Sky you get a lot more.
Good points and bad points about TV
Some is nonsense and some is reality.
It rules your life.
You just sit and stare.
Instead you could be out and about
Doing things you've always wanted to do.
Not just watching a box without a care.
Dare yourself to go somewhere.

Jaclyn Thomas (13)
Heath Comprehensive School

WALKING ALONG THIS BUSY LONDON STREET!

As I walk along this busy London street,
I see homeless people,
Huddled, begging at my feet.
From shop doorways to street corners,
They're dotted about,
Unwanted and hungry,
They live in doubt.
I stop and wonder,
What life do these people hold,
Why do they choose to live like this?
Maybe they had trouble at home or just couldn't take it anymore.
As I walk along this busy London street,
I see a man curled up on his sleeping bag like a squirrel hibernating in
winter.

He looks cold and hungry.
He suddenly notices me and looks at me as if I'm wanted for murder,
I feel guilty so I pop some coins in his tin
I look him in the eyes only to see heartache
But he looks at me and I quickly turn away feeling embarrassed,
I now feel a hard lump in my throat,
Maybe a sign of uneasiness,
So I smile and quickly walk away only to see more homeless
People begging along this busy London street.

Laura McGimpsey (14)
Heath Comprehensive School

MY WORLD

In the classroom I sit and stare,
Into my little world I glare,
Baking hot sand
Shining sea,
This is where I wish to be.

In the classroom I sit and stare,
Into my little world I glare,
Screaming crowds,
Rain pouring on me,
This is where I'd wish to be.

Sadie Blythe (12)
Heath Comprehensive School

SYDNEY OLYMPICS 2000!

Far on the other side of the world,
The Olympic Games have begun,
It starts with a man who carries
A torch comes to the end of his run.

They light a great lamp that burns
All the time up in the Australian sky
It shines all the time that the
Teams and the flags of the nations
That take part march by.

With all the spectators watching on
The athletes compete to be the best
To see how many medals can be won
They'll run, jump, sail and swim to
Beat the rest.

When the games are over, the people
Will go home,
The giant torch will stop burning
And in four years time - at Athens
The flame again is burning.

Heather Birmingham (11)
Heath Comprehensive School

ADDICTIVE TELEVISION

Television rules family life,
They gape at the screen,
And waste ten years of their life,
They sit and watch some woman
Or fella in a wooden box,
We loll and slop and lounge about,
And stare until our eyes pop out,
Sound up, sound down,
Whichever you prefer,
A price to pay for BBC1 and 2,
ITV as free as can be.

Gemma Leach (13)
Heath Comprehensive School

TELEVISION

If there was no television
You would get out and about
Going places, seeing places
Not just wishing you were there
Television rules your life
Just sitting there while your eyeballs pop in and out
Television wrecks your lives
So get out and enjoy yourselves
In nearly every house I've seen
They have had the silly box around.

Vicki Wood (13)
Heath Comprehensive School

TELEVISION

Enjoyable, relaxing, entertaining and cheap,
People are looking, taking a peep.
You're looking there, gazing at it,
Pull the plug and that will be it.
Looking at the big blank screen,
Always giving it a thorough clean.
Putting the magic box back on,
Oh no, the electricity's gone.
Everyone panics, everyone screams,
Here comes the light beams.
Switch on the television, yes it works.
Everyone is happy, everyone cheers,
Let's watch the footie and have a few cheers.

Daniel Parkinson (13)
Heath Comprehensive School

TELEVISION

Television is cool,
I watch it every day after school
I turn it off,
But just for tea,
Then it's all I see,
My mum goes mad,
It's not fair!
She says my eyes will go square,
But what's the difference?
. . . I don't care!

Sarah Carter (13)
Heath Comprehensive School

TELEVISION

Television is what we blame
For bringing all of us to shame
It clogs and clutters up the mind
It really makes us dull and blind
We stare and sit and loll and slop
Until we really just lost the plot

My name, my parents scream and shout
I can't help if the lights have gone out
The volume's high, I sit and stare
Oh my God, my eyes have gone square

Television is what we blame
For making us all go insane
We sit and stare and loll and slop
Until we really just lost the plot.

Lisa Gavin (13)
Heath Comprehensive School

TELEVISION

I used to sit and watch and stare,
At the television set just sitting there.
I'd watch the programmes
Over and over,
Till my mum said 'Oh, give over'
You loll and slop
Until your eyeballs nearly pop.
'Neighbours' is really cool,
I got bored staying in school,
I watch TV all the time,
This might end up being a crime.

Laura Bate (13)
Heath Comprehensive School

TELEVISION

It kills imagination dead
It blows up in your head
Pull the plug and it'll be dead
The brain becomes as soft as cheese
You go all wobbly at the knees

Watch the footy, watch the games
Watch the big names play the games
Your eyes become square
If you glare

Puts light into your life
When it is dull
If you are grumpy
It keeps you company.

Mathew Booth (13)
Heath Comprehensive School

TELEVISION

TV blows
TV sucks
The TV set beats every bet
Hypnotic waves
Out the screen
We are watching Mr Bean
Kills the senses
Dims the brain
Makes a child dumb and lame
Destroys friends
Destroys bends
We can watch it till the end.

Daniel Sankey (13)
Heath Comprehensive School

THE BOOK BREW

Books they come and books they go,
A witches cauldron and a dead man's toe,
Hubble, bubble, adventure and trouble,
Mystery, fantasy or history on the double.

Now add colour and detailed text,
Add danger and mystery which go in next,
Then crime or murder for excellence
And funny bits, cliffhangers or suspense.

Books are funny and books are dreams,
Pictures in your head is what it seems,
So mix in some feelings, some romance or terror,
Stir up some clues, plots or a dilemma

I wish a book would never end,
But when it does, I'm sure there's some you could lend.

Pick books up and put them back,
Because books they come and books they go,
They're everywhere in libraries,
Just search high and low.

Laura Lacey (11)
Heath Comprehensive School

A THANK YOU POEM TO SANTA

Thanks for that the reindeer ring,
Thanks for all the toys you bring,
Thanks for the winds that blow
And thanks for the skies that snow.

Thanks for reindeer that eat my carrot,
Thanks for giving people a parrot,
Thanks for eating my mince pie,
I wish you'd write a letter goodbye.

Thanks for climbing down the chimney
And for all the presents that you bring me,
I hope I have been good,
So I can eat the Christmas pud.

Thanks for all the things you do,
No child will go boo, hoo, hoo,
When you come I won't go boo
And thanks for just being you.

Tom Hulse (11)
Heath Comprehensive School

A DOSSER'S LIFE

You're sprawled on the concrete floor, the wind stinging your skin,
No energy to beg, plead or cry.
So you bury your head in your rags with shame,
That's a dosser's life, a dosser's life.

Passers-by avoid you, or stare like you're an animal in the zoo.
Nobody else knows how low you can feel,
So dirty, alone and scared.
That's a dosser's life, a dosser's life.

Fighting back the tears that sting your eyes like 1000 pins,
Your matted hair straggled across your face,
Your hands scratched and sore.
Your stomach so empty it feels like a gigantic pit . . .
A dosser's life, a dosser's life.

Something deep inside you, a little light of hope,
Helps you to bare the hunger, the anxiousness and the cold,
But only for a little while,
Soon, that light will go out, fade away . . .
That's a dosser's life, a dosser's life.

Wendy Osborne (13)
Heath Comprehensive School

LOVE

Love is red,
It smells like roses
And looks like chocolate,
Love tastes like strawberries and cream,
It sounds like a dancing honeybee
And is shaped like a heart.

Love lives in your heart,
It's always warm
And it feels like silk and velvet.

Love is sweet,
Everyone likes it
And they think it's beautiful.

Kayleigh McMillan (11)
Heath Comprehensive School

THE CLOWN

Clowns are funny,
They have red noses,
They have huge pants,
Clowns are funny,
They have giant shoes,
They throw pies at each other,
Clowns are funny
They ride fat bikes
And thin bikes
They juggle eggs
And plates,
Clowns are funny.

Joanne Illidge (11)
Heath Comprehensive School

I WISH . . .

I wish I were a bird
So I could fly right up to the sky,
To sing sweetly and softly
To the people down below.

I wish I were a cat
So I could go anywhere I wanted
And curl up by the fire
And sleep till night ends.

I wish I were a dog
So I could roam and groan
And bark at the people passing by
And to chew upon my bone.

I wish I were a hamster,
So I could sleep in my warm bed
And complete the course of my toys
And eat my food quickly so no one else can.

Hayley Gavin (11)
Heath Comprehensive School

DAYS

Days go by very fast,
Days are like the winter at last,
They come and go every day,
Which makes them more thought of
In a way.

Siobhan Gibbons (11)
Heath Comprehensive School

IF I COULD BE . . .

If I could be an animal,
Just for one day,
I'd be a bird and fly up, up away.

I'd like to see the rooftops, that I wouldn't normally see,
Of the houses and buildings
That are higher than me.

I would fly through the clouds,
That I wouldn't usually do,
From up there I'd be able to see you.

I wouldn't get tired when I'm flying around,
I'd laugh at the traffic queues,
Down on the ground.

I would build a nice nest so cosy and warm,
To keep me safe from any storm.

The only thing that worries me is what I'd eat for my tea,
I'd drink the dewdrops off the plants
And look at worms with a glance.

The thought of eating them for tea,
Makes me glad that I'm still me.

Nicola Johnston (11)
Heath Comprehensive School

HARRY POTTER HAIKU

He lives with his aunt
His name is Harry Potter
He went to Hogwarts.

It was a castle
With many cold corridors
And a gamekeeper.

His name was Hagrid
He had a massive dragon
His name was Norbert.

Harry loves Hogwarts
But if you want to find more
Read Harry Potter!

Roxanne Philip (12)
Heath Comprehensive School

AS I SIT

As I sit in my stone doorway
  I gaze at people passing by
    Waiting for the light of day
      Life just makes me want to cry
        As I sit in my stone doorway . . .

Walking down a one-way street
  My skin tingles against the cold
    Nowhere to go, no one to meet
      This young soul is getting old
        Walking down a one-way street . . .

I ask for a little change
  But people detour round my path
    They will never change their ways
      Just because I need a bath
        I ask for a little change . . .

As I dream in my stone doorway
  I see people helping my cause
    Waiting for the light of day
      Hope opens invisible doors
        All as I sit in my stone doorway . . .

Nicola Griffiths (13)
Heath Comprehensive School

SEA CREATURES

The sea was rough,
The waves were high,
The clouds were racing,
Though the sky
And every creature in the sea
Was just as frightened as can be.

Can you see them hidden there?
A mermaid with her seaweed hair,
A crab with his hard rock shell,
A lobster and some shrimps as well.

An octopus with his big round head,
A starfish with his fingers spread,
They're hidden there for you to spy,
You'll find them if you really try.

Becky Barber (11)
Heath Comprehensive School

IF I COULD BE A BIRD FOR A DAY

If I could be an animal for a day,
I'd be a bird and fly away,
Up into the clear blue sky,
Higher and higher I'd go,
Look over trees and fields,
While I have the world at my feet,
I'd go into the clouds,
With the sun burning hard,
As my feathers are sleek.

Sara Holt (11)
Heath Comprehensive School

MY DAD'S COOKING

My dad is Nick,
He cooks all the food
And when I come to taste it,
It makes me feel sick.
When my dad Nick is
Cooking it always breaks my heart,
Especially when he adds beans
That's the yucky part!
So now you know my dad Nick,
He really is a twerp!
I really hate his cooking,
It always makes me burp!
Oops!

Zoe Richards (11)
Heath Comprehensive School

LIVERPOOL LFC

Liverpool are the best, the very best,
Michael's fast you must not blink!
He is quicker than you think,
Robbie Fowler he's our prowler,
Just you watch, he'll score a growler.

Liverpool are back, trying their best,
Just believe us, we'll beat the rest,
If you want to see how good they are
Come to Anfield, it's not that far.

Chelsea, Man Utd, Leeds too,
Watch your back because we will beat you.

Anthony Myers (11)
Heath Comprehensive School

THE SOUNDS OF A WATERFALL

I like the sound of a waterfall
Just like my dad's shower
In the hall
It can be small
It can be tall
But I like the sound of a waterfall.

Splashing sounds hit the ground
Water, water all around
On the floor,
Or on the wall,
But I still like the sound of a waterfall.

Waterfall on the rocks
Shall I wash my vest and socks?
Wet my hair,
Wash my face
I think waterfalls are ace.

Noisy but nice,
Water like ice,
Looking and listening,
To what you could be missing,
A waterfall,
Or my dad's hall
But I still like the sound of a waterfall.

Alex Parsons (11)
Heath Comprehensive School

THE WIND

I stood amongst the trees
The wind around me was a breeze.
I followed the winding path so steep
Into the forest so deep.
There I met a man who blew
The wind around me that was so cold.
I asked him why he blew so strong
He told me it was his job for so long.
He told me he started when he was four
But now he looked a thousand or more.
He told me he would pass his job on
To his son I presume when his time come.
Tell me he said in a croaky voice,
How would you get home if you had a choice?
I would like to go like a shot
Above the trees and chimney pots
He told me to close my eyes, with hand on heart
The wind he blew was just a fart.
His age was showing, I had to laugh
I said I would walk back along the path.

Louise Berry (11)
Heath Comprehensive School

POEM

When the sky turns orange in the morning light,
When the moon is lit in the middle of the night,
When the children are playing in the street,
While the adults are always on their feet.
People are doing their jobs all day,
While people are living their lives away.

Rebecca Jones (11)
Heath Comprehensive School

A PICNIC WITH WINNIE

I'm having a picnic with Winnie the Pooh,
Piglet, Eeyore and Tigger too!
Roo is picking pink and blue flowers,
The sun has been shining brightly for hours,
Piglet is hiding away from me,
Oh there he is behind that tree!
Winnie is eating all the honey,
Tigger's jokes are hilariously funny.
Rabbit is laughing with Eeyore and I,
As Christopher Robin watches bees buzz by.
This picnic has been extremely good,
The best ever picnic in Hundred Acre Wood!

Sarah Hoyland (12)
Heath Comprehensive School

TELEVISION

Television is the bomb,
That's why . . .
I sit in front and turn it on.
Both me and my family think
It's cool,
Before and after work and school,
I watch it all the time,
That's why my mum always whines.
It makes me laugh,
It makes me cry,
So that's the truth, I wouldn't lie.
If I had to choose,
The television wouldn't lose!

Victoria Stanley (13)
Heath Comprehensive School

MY ROOM

My room is up in the loft
And my bed is really soft,
I have everything I need,
Except for my feed
And for that I go downstairs.

In my room I have loads of great stuff
And I go up there when I get in a huff,
Especially when my sisters annoy me,
I stay up there until tea
And for that I go downstairs.

I like to watch my television
And now and then do some revision,
I look through my window at the stars,
Then I think I need a Mars
And for that I go downstairs.

Jamie Caza (11)
Heath Comprehensive School

THE SMARTIE

A shiny sun shaped object,
Landed on my desk,
It looks like a button
And feels like a gem.
It smells like melting chocolate,
Melting by the sun,
The shiny sun shaped object,
Has formed a little puddle,
Of melting chocolate,
In the middle of my desk.

Stacey Johnson (12)
Heath Comprehensive School

THE POLO

It tastes as sharp as a kitchen knife,
Stabbing you with an injection of flavour,
It is a cold cube of ice bouncing around
Your mouth.

It looks like a rubber ring made of white clouds,
Peaceful and calm.
It is a white snake coiled up asleep.

It smells cool like the Arctic
White across ice ridden plains,
It is a refreshing zesty lime.

It feels smooth like the ocean on a calm day,
Relaxed, silent and still,
It is a tight, leather-backed book.

Tom Morris (12)
Heath Comprehensive School

SCHOOL

School starts in autumn,
Ends in July,
Breaks in the middle.

Oh thank God at last,
Summer is here,
No more teachers,
No more fears.

Back again,
For a whole new year,
Oh at last a break is here.

Kelly Gleave (12)
Heath Comprehensive School

AUTUMN

Leaves seemed to wither away,
Never managed to fight another day,
The wind howled lifting their leaves,
Almost reviving their life.

Swallows flew all heading south,
All the insects got caught in their mouth,
When it warmed up they would return.

Mr Frost froze everywhere,
Making everything hard and cold,
When the sun came out to dance,
The frost would have no chance.

The squirrel came out to collect a meal,
From a friend he may steal,
Nuts and big acorns,
'Yum! Yum! Yum!' he thought.
'All this food to fill my tum!'

Hayley Mountford (12)
Heath Comprehensive School

MY DOG HOLLY

I have a dog called Holly,
She means the world to me and
Every time I see her, she is always ever
So jolly to see.
She would jump up high, up on my knee
And lick my face with so much glee.
Then I would sit on the floor and
Play tug of war and probably get knocked over.

Lindsey Gittins (12)
Heath Comprehensive School

MARTIANS MADE ON MARS

Walking along the street last night,
Eyes upon the stars,
This made me wonder,
If beyond the yonder,
Was there life on Mars?

Although I cannot see them,
Dancing on the stars,
Or playing Martian tennis
Or driving wacky cars.

I used my imagination,
But all that I could see,
Were minute blobs of aliens
Waving down at me.

So I jumped in my rocket
And glided into space
So all the groovy Martians
Could see my handsome face.

The aliens were fluffy
With little diamond eyes
Oh no it's getting darker
Time to say goodbyes.

So again I boarded my rocket
And soared amongst the stars,
Now I know the real truth
There is life on Mars.

David Tomlinson (12)
Heath Comprehensive School

I Am What I Am

I am an old teapot
Once I was used at every tea party,
Steaming uncontrollably inside,
My shining china handle
Polished every day
Proudly I stood on the table,
While the cups and saucers turned away,
I had my own little cupboard where no other
China could stay,
My own thought was that I was special,
Better than the rest,
But now I am ruined,
When the grandchildren came to stay,
I was dropped and cracked down the middle
And never the same again.
I am dusty and in a dark cupboard,
In the corner where no one can see,
I feel ashamed and embarrassed
For I feel not like the special me,
Soon I will be put in the garbage
And I will be no more,
No shining china teapot
Just a crack upon the floor.

Stacey Malvern (12)
Heath Comprehensive School

THE TEDDY BEAR

I am an old teddy bear,
Once I was in my prime,
My soft brown fur lovely to touch,
My black beady eyes sparkling in the moonlight
And my dazzling smile stretched across my face,
Who could have a better teddy bear than me?
I used to sit on top of bed watching
The days and nights pass by,
Now I lie under it waiting for my
Owner to find me.
My fur is all knotted,
My eyes are all misty
And my arms and legs have nearly
Fallen off.
How I wish I could go back to the
Old times when I would be taken around
Everywhere and held tight by my owner,
Now those days are gone.
Soon I will be thrown out into the rubbish
And left waiting and waiting for somebody
Else to find me.

Nicole Schofield (12)
Heath Comprehensive School

MY LIFE

My worries lie behind me,
My goals are in front,
My pleasures lie around me,
My mind is high above.

My age is young,
My mind is bold,
My head is full,
Of knowledge new and old.

Thomas Smith (13)
Heath Comprehensive School

THE DARK INSIDE

The intruder slithered within my chest,
Its darkened soul attacked my mind.
The lifeless entity withdrew its fangs,
To coil up and shrivel and die.
Atop the hill, the demon stirred,
Its lifelong pet no longer heard.
I'd killed its creature, I'd killed its creation,
With my marvellous soul of good.
His urge for vengeance, his need for wrath,
Dominated what little soul he had.
He trekked the journey towards his home,
In the satanic fires of Hell, his mind
Consumed by revenge.
I turned, disgusted to see him leave,
As his mortal enemy arose victorious.
Alas, on the day of my victory, the creature
Soon returned, its dark mind set on destruction.
As I drowned in pain and fear of death,
I saw the demon again.
His face evil and twisted, his eyes
Non-existent, I lived in fear of him.

Ashley Ettrick (12)
Heath Comprehensive School

INJURY RICK

There was a boy called Rick,
Who was always being sick,
He throws up in sinks and many bowls,
His bed covers are covered with holes.

He then fell down the stairs,
With an unhealthy tear,
The ambulance came and took him away,
To the hospital where he could stay.

The doctor told him to stay calm,
He had only broken his arm,
Then he went to the caster,
To heal the injury a lot faster.

That's one story of injury Rick,
He still, is always being sick,
I wonder how the poor boy thinks,
We guess he is a real jinx.

David Mayock (12)
Heath Comprehensive School

SCHOOLED FOR LIFE

I think school is great,
I have done well,
But at the end of the day,
I can't wait for the bell.

I'm not into tests,
Though I'm one of the best,
So when I go home,
I just want a rest.

Philip Light (12)
Heath Comprehensive School

MY GRANDAD

He has wisps of hair,
Like high fluffy clouds that are blown by the wind,

He has sophisticated glasses,
That make him look like a
Rocket scientist.

He has a fondness for gardening,
Rather like
Alan Titchmarsh.

He loves a tot of whisky,
As a night cap,
So he says,

He strolls around at Maybecks
Looking for adders and wildlife,
Sometimes getting lucky.

He rustles up curries,
That tickle your tastebuds
And sometimes,
Burn them,

His smile is like
The man on the moon
And his jolly character,

Reminds me of
Saint Nick,
I'm so chuffed that he's my grandad.

David Horsley (13)
Knutsford High School

A BOAT ODYSSEY

The boat safely set out to sea,
We all said our goodbyes,
The captain asked us all to stand aside.

The ocean was a clear blue colour,
We all saw the lighthouse flashing in the distance,
I could see the people waving us goodbye,
I was living my dream!

I could smell the scent of fish,
The captain told us all to stop the boat,
We put the anchor down and started fishing,
Jimmy caught the biggest.

The captain stopped the boat for a while,
I looked above at the sky, it was a dreamy blue,
It made me think of home.

Set sail again
A tropical sunset was ahead of us,
But not for long.

The boat was swaying from side to side,
Rain was coming in as fast as lightning,
Waves were crashing against the boat.

Shouting was coming from around the boat,
I looked around and saw people running to help,
'Come on' I heard, I saw a misty, old figure standing
In front of me.

I heard thunder and saw lightning coming from above,
The sky was grey and cold,
It sent a shiver down my spine.

It died down slowly as we went south,
We made it!
A happy ending at last.

Sophie Norman (13)
Knutsford High School

AMUSED TO DEATH

Inspiration,
Is the hardest thing to find,
In a world so dead, only the haunting rhyme
Of a spirit or so once it was,
Twisted and tortured, humans recklessly called 'God.'
Oh he was a poet, the best the world had seen,
But his disturbing behaviour less than put everyone at ease,
They whispered uncomfortably 'What does he mean?'
'Oh,' he cried 'Why are you so dumb?'
'Can't you see the irresistible wicked pun?'
It killed him in the end, he dragged the world down too,
Spinning until twisted,
Twisted, until bitter,
Bitter until devilish, the cold, harsh end
And of course, it amused him to death.

Charlotte Mann (13)
Knutsford High School

FAINT

Just a whisper,
Faint,
Only a dream you say,
The smiling politicians,
Covering it up,
'So glad it's not me'
'Can't be that bad'
And the truth?
Devastating,
Who cares?

Just a whisper against the powers,
But still there,
It's not our fault,
We're too faint,
Got the numbers, not the power.

Who cares?
Not you, not anyone,
It's all a mask.
Poverty wields its net and pulls us in.
Who cares?
We do,
Not you in your business suit,
Or you taking your child to school,
We do but it's not enough,
Too faint.

Holly Poynton (13)
Knutsford High School

FEELINGS

Dolphins playing till they have no energy,
Large noise coming towards them is a ferry,
The ferry is going to Spain,
The sun and the bright warm colours reflect off the dolphins,
Remembering my bedroom I am leaving behind,
Hoping we have a nice villa to live in and shops to go to,
The bright clear blue sea,
Feeling empty but something troubling me,
Dreaming of being hurt or someone close that I can see,
And yet colourful light dreams,
Waiting, waiting, for the bad 2000 year to die.

Helen Roberts (13)
Knutsford High School

SUNSET SCENE

Yellow lifts the world
Warming in the gentle heat.
Orange colours the Earth
Softening and caring.
Fiery red makes the sky angry
Leaving the circling birds
Black and empty.
Purple covers like a blanket
Making the world seem safe and secure.
Black washes over dark and menacing,
With little bright sparks to light its path.

Sarah Mason (13)
Knutsford High School

THE MACHINE OF LIFE

Ill, poor people by the hundred,
All the beds were nearly full,
While outside, the night sky thundered
The atmosphere was dull,
The machines bleeped,
Staff scurried about,
While people were asleep
Hardly making any sound.

We're losing him! Quick guys! An ecstasy of fumbling
They got the equipment just in time,
Some still hurrying and stumbling,
I wish his end could have been mine,
I heard the machines,
The rustling of hard working souls,
Mixed in were the distant screams,
Like tunnelling moles, they had their goals . . .

He was gone,
My only son,
I wish there was something I could have done,
My life I know will not be fun,
I turned my back and walked away,
All I knew,
Was that tomorrow would bring another day.

Rebecca Weston (13)
Knutsford High School

BEHIND THE BOOK COVER . . .

Loyal eyes,
A heart of stone,
A lovely house,
A lonely home.

A charming smile,
Uneasy words,
A mind of secrecy,
Seldom heard.

A comforting hand,
With a hidden grasp
Eternal love,
Not made to last.

A truthful voice,
Always near a lie,
Like a shining star,
Always near the sky.

A charming friend,
But a fiend too much,
In a summer's world,
Is a frosty touch.

Alice Pemberton (13)
Knutsford High School

AN ODYSSEY TO DEATH

The beginning is born and a journey dies
A whole life ahead - no fears, no lies.

For now is the start, a life has begun
Nothing else matters but health, joy and fun.

A few years on, nothing is the same
Making lots of mistakes with no one to blame.

What is the point? You live then you die,
Why go through the heartache, why even try?

A chapter ends and another starts
Adulthood beckons, adolescence departs.

Light at the end of the tunnel for you
Smile at the hard times and love will see you through.

Now is the start, this is your time
A big wide world, you're in your prime.

Some live to work, some work to live,
Nurture the good, the bad - forget and forgive.

Time goes quicker, stairs seem steeper,
Memory may fail but memories grow deeper.

Close your eyes, your life on earth is done,
For when you awake a new life will have begun.

The beginning is born and a journey dies,
A new life ahead, no fears, no lies.

Felicity Hutcheson (14)
Knutsford High School

SEEING DOUBLE

I have a baby, but not one, two that are as one,
Am I seeing double?
A haze, a haze of tubes and machines surround my little angels.
Am I seeing double?
'They are sharing a heart and lungs' they tell me.
No I tell them, they have them each.
They say I'm seeing double.
Am I seeing double?
What is a heart, a pair of lungs, to decide my daughter's destiny?
I ask God, am I seeing double?
I cannot hear a reply.
Has he forgotten me?
Am I seeing double?
Am I hearing nothing than that solitary heartbeat?

Kathryn Harrison (13)
Knutsford High School

POEM IN OCTOBER

Leaves are dropping, conkers are falling,
October must be here.
Red, brown, white - all of the colours,
October must be here.
The sun is dropping, it's getting colder,
October must be here.
The moon is shining bright in the morning,
October must be here.
Rain falling down from the sky,
October must be here.
Soon Christmas will arrive in Winter,
And October will be gone.

Andrew Davies (13)
Longdendale High School

MR KANTOFFEL

Mr Kantoffel went crazy,
His wife, her name Daisy.
She left him on his own
For the fit binman Jone.
He could not cut his own nails
And all he could make were snails.
He could not wash his vest
So you could see his hairy chest.
He had smelly shoes
And he drank loads of booze.
He was drunk all the time
So he turned to a life of crime.
He was out on the street,
So he stole some meat.
When he was caught
His house was bought.
He got put in jail
But was let out on bail.
So he stole some coal
And was thrown in a hole.
That was the end of Mr Kantoffel.

Ryan Moyles (12)
Longdendale High School

A WAR POEM

Think of all the horrible things,
that war can bring and show
Think of how the families cope,
and the way they have to go

Think of the very brave soldiers,
who faced the blood and gore
Think of all the friends they lost
and the families they remember

So on Remembrance Sunday,
spare two minutes to show
How you remember the soldiers,
who fought in all the wars.

Stephen Maher (11)
Longdendale High School

THE BRIDGE

The summer sun reflects on the small little stream,
Tinkle, tinkle, is the noise of a nearby miniature waterfall.

As you walk making noises on the roof which shelters the old cows,
They start to moan which drives us demented.

Every step across the span,
Spying on the sparrows that dance at the bank,
With every ripple from the smooth, gentle wind,
Comes a new, hop, skip or jump.

Many people travel day by day not viewing the site in the
                                        appropriate manner.

The grass is fresh with dew on the tips,
Flowers sway from side to side feeling happy,
Full of joy.

One step,
Two steps, and at last we have finally finished.
The spectacular view is complete.
You see far and wide from all angles.

The summer sunset fades away,
Behind the hills, behind the valleys.

Hannah Searle (13)
Longdendale High School

ACROSTIC POEMS

T he tree is being stripped of leaves,
R ight down to its branches,
E ach branch has no leaves,
E veryday is on the ground.

L ight, crispy, brown leaves,
E ach leaf on the ground,
A brown leaf just falling,
F alling slowly down to the earth.

W et and damp,
E very day the same,
A n occasional day it's not wet,
T he days are all just dull,
H eat off the bonfire,
E veryone around,
R ight around the fire.

S o cloudy and dull,
K notted round with clouds,
Y ellow leaves swirling around.

R ain falling all the time,
A ll the time it falls,
I t falls all day long,
N ever does it stop falling.

Lee Robertson (12)
Longdendale High School

SHAPE POETRY

The Davis Cup final starts
It's Henman Sampras
England America
It's the best final ever seen
As the game begins
Each on the other side of the court
And gets it to 15-0
As the game gets further and further
Sampras keeps getting better and better
Sampras wins sets 1+2
Henman comes back to win 3+4
As the 5th set begins
The crowd becomes louder and louder
The players become more nervous than ever
But the games keep getting better and better
Henman serves the first game
Henman wins the point
Henman wins the game
Henman's now the favourite to win
Which helps Sampras become more unsettled
But Sampras comes back to win the next game
The game then ends at 6 games all
And a tie-break to decide who wins all
Sampras in the end wins the cup
And lifts the trophy for his country
With Henman losing for his country
He throws his racket into the crowd
And then walks off not at all proud.

Mark Foote (12)
Longdendale High School

CRICKET

Bowl
Hit
Six
Run
Bowl
Hit
Caught
Out!
Change
Six!
The bowler
bowls the ball.
It bounces down
The wicket. The
batsman hits the
ball. The ball sails
over the first fielder
but is caught by the
next. The bowler
celebrates, he has
taken a wicket. The
batsman has to change.
DF
Duncan Fearnly.

Adam Gee (12)
Longdendale High School

THE MOUSE

I know a little mouse,
he lives under the stairs,
he runs across the room at night
to see who he can scare.

He makes my mother scream,
he makes my sister cry,
he doesn't bother me at all,
I don't know why.

I give him bits of cheese,
and bits of bread and ham,
but the thing that he likes most of all
is a plate of strawberry jam.

Jodie Wilde (12)
Longdendale High School

HOMELESS

I am homeless
No one cares.

I have no money
No one cares.

I look scruffy
No one cares.

I sleep on the street
No one cares.

I die . . .
And no one cares!

Niall Fawcett (13)
Longdendale High School

BIRDS

The bird is flying in the sky,
near the treetops way up high
and all the time I wonder why,
how it is that birds can fly.

He leaves his nest to stretch his wings,
to hunt for worms and food and things,
the wind is strong, not much to find,
people throw bread, they are kind.

Winter comes, he feels the cold,
this tiny bird, he's growing old,
a house martin should migrate,
he wasn't strong enough. It's too late.

Claire Aitken (12)
Longdendale High School

SUN/CLOUD

Sun

The sun is shining, it's big and fat
Down on the grass is where we are sat
It makes all the things look happy and bright
What would happen without any light?

Cloud

A cloud floats all fluffy and light
Drifting along on a dark, starry night
Cupids and cherubs rest their wings
An angel, she's beautiful and she sings.

Cathryn Kidd (13)
Longdendale High School

LIMERICKS

A man once wanted to start stalking,
because he always liked walking.
he travelled on foot,
and never did tut,
but he never could stop talking.

A man once never ate meat,
unless it was charcoaled cows' feet,
and only green veg,
that was picked near a hedge,
otherwise he would never eat.

There once was a man called Vandam,
who liked eating mint sauce and lamb,
until one day,
he was strolling away,
and he walked into an angry ram.

Renée Fleming (12)
Longdendale High School

CONKERS

C onkers lying on the ground,
O nly the biggest and best around,
N o conkers in their shells,
K ids ringing the church bells,
E nd of the day, children are fighting,
R umours of conkers have spread,
S pring Avenue is their home,
   It's time to go to bed.

Danielle Hinchliffe (12)
Longdendale High School

THE BRIDGE

'Help, help!' the words still ring in my head!
'Help, help,' something that best friends dread.
I saw her falling, falling down, it suddenly seems
                            quiet in this town.
People say you've got to carry on,
but 'How?' I ask them, when my best friend's gone.
I try to think of the good points, how she had that special way.
But it's hard to think of the good points when you remember
                            that fateful day.
She never did anything wrong, never would think of it
But it was she who had to pay the price and fall to the
                  bottom of that endless, water-filled pit!
I've never been superstitious,
In fact I've talked about it, I've been quite malicious.
But I wish that day I'd found a four-leafed clover,
Before she slipped and went over!

Jennifer Bennett (12)
Longdendale High School

HOMELESSNESS

The rain hammers down,
Again, again and again.

I try to stay warm but the cold has me.
It holds me in its icy grip.
I twist and turn but no, I cannot escape now
I am drifting . . . into eternal warmth . . .

David Batty (14)
Longdendale High School

THE HOMELESS - WHO'S GONNA HELP THEM?

I was walking down a street,
When a weak figure caught my eye.
There he was, in old rags
Just waiting for someone to give him some change.
But, instead all he got were nasty comments
And dirty looks,
As if he had no right at all to be there,
Asking for someone to help.
He wasn't alone either,
There sitting with him was a little dog to
                              keep him company,
Also wrapped in rags, to keep him warm.
They both looked as if they hadn't eaten in days,
And no one would give them anything.
But if we won't help them, who will?

Jaime Elizabeth Briggs (13)
Longdendale High School

THE WINTER

The winter is coming closer every second,
The wind howling like a wolf on the
Top of a mountain.
The rain coming down, splashing on the
Cold, wet, hard, concrete surface.
The snow drifting down, then melting
Into nothing when it hits the surface.
The winter is going away,
Away, away.

Paul McClusky (13)
Longdendale High School

HOMELESSNESS POEM

I sit in my battered cardboard box - my home,
My shell to protect me from the outside world.
I peer over the edge of the thick, brown corrugation.
At all the people who have homes to go to when it's
          rainy and windy, in the warm out of the cold.

I think about how they have a nice, cosy, soft, warm bed.
And how I have a dirty, cold, hard, uncomfortable pavement.
You're lucky to get an hour's sleep out here.

From here I can see a fast-food place,
The red and yellow sign, warmly illuminated against the dark.
From my safe haven, my cardboard box.
I can see through the sparkling, shiny windows,
Revealing endless white-tiled flooring and white tables -
I wish I was there now.

But I wouldn't fit in.
With my dirty rags and my thick, uncut hair and beard.
I'm different - you make me different,
And I always will be different - without your help.
Please help me, I beg you to help me -
But you won't help me.
So now, for as long as I live - I will be condemned to my safe haven,
My four walls of corrugation.

Bill Kalaher (14)
Longdendale High School

HOMELESSNESS

Cold, cold to the bone
But no shelter from the cold
No one to care for
No one to share with
Nothing to eat
No drink to drink
Nothing to call mine except a cardboard box
And a tattered old blanket to keep me warm

I have no choice
It's my way of life
With no one to laugh with
No one to cry with
No money to buy things
No address to give out
Nothing to call mine except a cardboard box
And a tattered old blanket to keep me warm

You wouldn't understand
What is important to you
Doesn't matter to me
Because I have no brothers to fight with
No sisters to shout at
I have been disowned
With nothing to call mine except a cardboard box
And a tattered old blanket to keep me warm.

Heather Tolley (13)
Longdendale High School

DID YOU HELP ME?

I had no place to go
No family, no friends,
I had nothing to my name

But did you help me?
Did you help me?

I was freezing
I was cold
I had no food, no drink

But did you help me?
Did you help me?

I slept in shop doorways
not sleeping any night
I was scared and I was frightened

But did you help me?
Did you help me?

I got beaten up last night
by some lager louts that were drunk
I was left there to bleed, I nearly died

But did you help me?

Rahaymin Chowdhury (13)
Longdendale High School

HOMELESSNESS

Cold, scared, vulnerable and lonely,
The fear's always there when there's nowhere to go to,
Wind blows, rain falls, you shiver all night,
The frightening feeling that really goes through you.

The minutes seem like hours and you wish it was morning,
As you're trying to sleep in your cardboard box or shop doorway,
You wish, you dream you could have a place just for tonight,
You think about the future, every day and all day.

And when tomorrow comes, it's just as miserable,
You spend it begging just to survive another day.
No one understands how it feels to be homeless,
Everyone just passes by, hoping you'll go away.

Ben Hope (13)
Longdendale High School

HOMELESSNESS!

H ope is the cushion I fall back on,
O ther people's faces staring and shrugging,
M oney is hard for me to get hold of,
E verlasting nights with no sleep in sight,
L onely faces are all I see in my reflection,
E very night my family passes in my thoughts,
S adness visits me every day,
S alty tears trickle down my cheek,
N ight-times I have as little as one hour's sleep,
E very second I am filled with fear,
S o many people give, and yet, so many don't,
S o the question is, would *you* help *me?*

Heather Morgan (13)
Longdendale High School

ESCAPE

I've seen the seasons come and go,
You walk by, with the people you know.
You look down to me, I'm a piece of dirt,
I must be a disease, you don't want to get hurt.

The frost burns into my tender feet,
People in warm coats wander down the street,
Am I invisible, a horrible sight
Or are you just ignorant when I'm alone in the night?

I hold in my hand the piece of dope,
It blocks things out, it helps me cope,
I know it sounds weak, but I have no hope.

As I drift away, I thank God it's my time,
As the church clock continues to chime,
My troubles are over, I'm free from the pain,
The fierce wind blows down the icy lane.

You still don't look, you still don't care,
But how would you feel if *you* were me?
Wanting just one thing,
To be free.

Sarah Bunyan (13)
Longdendale High School

A WAR POEM

The bloodstained grass,
The gassy smell in the air,
The soldiers dying a painful death,
The danger lurking in the air.

The gunshots firing,
The cries of pain,
The Commander crying,
'Shoot! Duck!'

I was standing on the grass,
Just waiting to be shot,
Watching people die a death,
I was next.

I was hiding in my trench,
Crying my eyes out,
Wanting to be back with my family,
The war, I *hate* it.

Francesca Davies (11)
Longdendale High School

WAR: THE REAL STORY

The sounds are horrible,
Loud shouting, screaming, *bang!*
My turn to shoot,
Oh no, get down.

I hate the war,
I'm bleeding too much.
Think my leg is broken,
It hurts a lot.

I want to go home,
It's cold and wet.
Stuck in this ditch.
'Go! Attack, attack, attack!'

I can't even move,
They're coming, I know.
Fighting, shooting, falling, dying,
War should be stopped,

Forever!

Stephanie Suthern (11)
Longdendale High School

A WAR POEM

A haunting noise
goes through my head,
of blasting cannons
and people dead.

Why did Americans
start this fight?
I wish they hadn't
and my decision is right.

At least my family
are safe at home,
but not I
I'm all alone.

Please someone help me
but who can?
Nobody's here
just a dead man.

A thundering bullet
goes through my heart,
is this the end?
Well, it's not the start.

I now die
upon this day,
November the 11th
I will go away.

Rebecca Bolton (11)
Longdendale High School

A POEM OF REMEMBRANCE

I can still hear the orders from the General to fire,
but mostly I can still hear the shots from the guns
and the troops' cries of pain.

I remember their pain etched on bloody faces,
their staring eyes whilst floating in knee-deep water,
the return fire from the hidden enemy somewhere in the dark,
sleeping in trenches with the stench of death on the freezing night air.

Suddenly, the declaration that the war was over, brought joy to all,
the shouts and cheers from the troops that remained are still heard,
arriving home brought tears of joy to my happy eyes,
hugs and kisses from family and loved ones eased painful memories.

Looking around, total devastation hit me,
the houses that once stood proud are all but gone
but a few are left standing amidst mountains of rubble and brick . . .

Emma Willingham (11)
Longdendale High School

HOMELESS

The homeless are people,
Through no choice of their own,
Are living on the streets,
Cold, hungry and alone.

In cardboard boxes, they sleep,
Doorways, parks and shelters,
No matter where they run,
Or what they become,
Please help these people.

Lewis Bradley (13)
Longdendale High School

WAR

I stand here
Khaki uniform
Itchy, crawling with lice
Boots caked in mud
Incessant rain
Leeching into my bones

I stand here
Shaking, drawing on my cigarette
Trying to stiffen my spine
With its noxious chemicals

I stand here
With my ears being assaulted
With terrifying screams of gunfire shells
And dying souls

I stand here
Trying to divorce myself
From my surroundings
Seeking in my mind
Comforting thoughts of home and
Treasured memories of past experiences

I stand here
Knowing I would rather
Stay here
In this filth and noise forever
Than go where I have to go

I stand here
And listen for the whistle
I climb the ladder
I run to the barbed wire
I feel the exhilaration
Of thinking I can survive this
Where others fall around me

I died here
A manic grin etched on my face
Did I die scared, mad or a hero?

Sasha Doherty (12)
Longdendale High School

WAR

The 11th of the 11th
Is such a sacred day
Our soldiers gave their
Lives without delay.

To save Europe from
Hitler's dark reign,
And keep burning
England's flame.

We wear poppies to show
Our love and care
For people who fought in
The polluted air.

The soldiers were young boys
Whose lives were lost
No time for teenage toys
Our freedom at such a cost.

We are grateful to them all
That they were so brave
No matter where they fall
Our future they did save!

Melissa Barker (11)
Longdendale High School

A WAR POEM

Gunshots from all around
Men either side of me wailing
The water is knee-high now
As we rest here, numb with pain

I fire my bullets with sorrow in my eyes
I can hear men screaming in the distance
Like me they are lonely
Like me they would rather die

I pull a picture from my muddy pocket
I miss my family
I guess that my friends have gone
How will I survive?

The war is over
Millions are dead
Husbands, wives, children, me
May they all rest in peace.

Amy Louise Noble (11)
Longdendale High School

A WAR POEM

I looked around,
What hell was brewing here,
Gunshots ringing in my ears,
Bloodstained troops lying all around.

But I had to keep going,
Keep on trying,
I think of my wife and children,
I would keep on going, for their sake.

The weak faces around me,
Our muddy clothes,
Not slept or washed in a week,
Not heard from home in months.

But people are depending on me,
The eyes of the world are on me,
I must carry on going,
I will fight this war till justice is done.

Rebecca Martens (12)
Longdendale High School

ALL AROUND

Blood spurting all around
People crying all around
Bombs blasting all around
Victory! Victory! Victory!
All around.

Planes flying all around
People screaming all around
Guns dropping all around
Surrender! Surrender!
All around.

Noises echoing all around
Deaf people all around
People falling all around
Death! Death! Death!
All around.

Lee Allcock (11)
Longdendale High School

THE FACES OF THE CHINA DOLLS

I had a dream,
That when I was little
My mum and dad
Came to take me to a nursery, but
They had cold, white faces,
Cold white hands,
Cold white hands clutched at mine.
I was taken to a grey building,
Under the stars.
A single corridor was lit.
Silhouettes of children ran,
Along it
With clattering footsteps.
I was strapped into a greasy uniform.
Inside it was hot,
There was a distant sound of
Crying,
I tried to peel the uniform off,
It was stuck.
I went into a grey
Carpeted room.
My parents had gone.
In front of me,
A little boy.
He was dressed as a sad clown,
Standing next to a pretend stove.
In the next room,
There was nothing.
A naked bulb,
Glared out of the dark.
In the corner,
A dusty staircase.

It led me down
To a terrible
Silent world.
A light flicked on.
I stared at rows of cages
Encasing real parents.
Mine were there.
They were real people.
Not the horrible china dolls,
With no feelings.
The room was filled with
Deafening roars
By a huge pick-up truck.
It churned
Down the stairs,
Chewing up clumps
Of plaster and wood.
Then it hit the floor.
Inside it I could see
The distant outline of
A white-coated doll.
It chewed up cages
One by one, then turned
And came
Towards . . .
        Me . . .

Alice Hyde (12)
Ryles Park County High School

NIGHTMARE ROLLER-COASTER

All my life has been a roller-coaster
It has its ups and downs
But mostly its ups.
It rolls for seven times,
Never knowing what is going to happen.
Sixteen jerks when it starts
Just like a baby trying to walk
And when it moves, it moves slowly
And then it speeds up and up
But then slows down as it comes to a drop,
A big, lonely drop.
I can hear the roller-coaster saying
'No, please, I don't want to go down that.'
It's just like me going to school.
But something or someone pushes it.
Screams are heard.
Just like me walking to school.

Claire Gatley (13)
Ryles Park County High School

THE SMALL BLACK BAT

There was a small, black bat,
small, round and furry, flying
through the dark black forest
searching for his juicy meal.

His dark, rubbery wings flap in the
smooth wind as he silently flies
through the sky.

Michael Clarke (14)
Ryles Park County High School

I FEEL EMPTY

Nothing is as lovely as the sound of a cry,
A cry of a child of your own.
When you hear you're pregnant,
With a child of your own
All you do is cry, a loving cry,
Although it's a long road,
Motherhood is the best thing,
It makes you laugh,
It makes you cry,
But in the end it's worth it,
Then you hear it's all a lie,
Your voice is no more,
You don't feel full,
You feel all your dreams are like glass,
Made to be broken,
It's then you feel empty,
Like you're nothing, no one.

Leanne Sarah Lee (13)
Ryles Park County High School

MUM

Just look at my mum, she is so funny
And all the time, she calls me Honey
Now and then she likes to cook
Every night, she reads me a book
To me and my brothers she is so kind
Today we left a mess and she did not mind
Everyone needs a mum as good as mine.

Gemma McDonald (13)
Ryles Park County High School

ALL THE WORLD'S A ROLLER-COASTER

All the world's a roller-coaster,
Life's full of ups and downs,
One minute you are smiling,
Then your face is full of frowns.
The playground is so boisterous,
It's a noisy rowdy patch,
I wish it could be more joyous,
We could have a friendly match.

Yes, the world's a roller-coaster,
It's full of ups and downs,
The visitors aren't smiling,
The teachers are full of frowns.
The children were all fooling,
'You really let us down!'
I wish there was just me,
I'd be as quiet as could be!

Luke Edwards (12)
Ryles Park County High School

LIFE IS LIKE A GAME

Life is like a game, you take control
You're like a player.
You're jumping over obstacles of life.
Another day is another level.
You start in a different way.
You never know what's round the corner
You start to worry
But when you face it
The worry goes away.
Life is like a game - you take control.

Lee Fitzgerald (12)
Ryles Park County High School

LIFE

Life has been like a roller-coaster
All the ups and downs of life
Sometimes I want to run and hide
Sometimes I want to take a peek
Of what's inside the book.
Some people have a brand new life
Some people's lives stay the same
Everyone is looking for something
But don't know where to start.
The roller-coaster can be scary at times
Like when you hurt yourself.
Some people can always play it cool
Like a log flume with water
Splashing in your face
But life is as simple as can be
So look after yourselves
And wait and see.

Sophie Hodkinson (13)
Ryles Park County High School

LIFE IS A GAME

Life is like a game,
It has its ups and downs,
Just like playing with a yo-yo,
It has its happy and sad times,
Just like winning or losing,
And that is why life is like a game.

Allan Alili (12)
Ryles Park County High School

THE PARANOID DREAM

The lady, she was mad
Not being mean, but she was.
She was manic depressive
Paranoid schizophrenic
She had a carer
A cautious man
Who treated her as a normal person.
The lady thought scary thoughts
And sometimes these things happened
She thought of assassination,
Screamed and jumped off her chair
The carer went over, with a bang, he was dead
The lady just sighed in despair
She left the door wide open.
The most wanted woman in the world
Left without a word.

Becky Trueman (12)
Ryles Park County High School

THE GAME

All my life has been a game
of laughter and sadness.
You never know what
might happen just around the corner.
Sometimes you can role a six
and move twice as fast.
But sometimes you just take
a chance and move a little slower.

Tara Bayley (12)
Ryles Park County High School

A DREAM OF SHADOWS

I picture my bedroom dark and cold
I see shadows moving across the walls
The moonlight shines in through the window
Casting a shadowy silhouette of a cat on the wall.
I can hear the chilly breeze rattling the window
Sending a chill down my spine.
I can hear the whispers of the wind,
Moaning and groaning, trying to get at me.
I feel frightened and trapped
I can't get out
The glass is beginning to break,
The voices will get at me soon.
Finally I wake up, that is my dream.

Lee Dixon (13)
Ryles Park County High School

FALLING

In my dreams I was falling,
Don't know where from.
Don't know where to,
Just falling, falling, falling.
Am I ever going to stop?
Then all of a sudden I wake up.
I go back to sleep and once again I start falling.
Don't know where from.
Don't know where to.
Just falling, falling, falling and waking up
                            again and again.
I carry on all night,
Just falling, falling, falling.

Wendy Bowyer (13)
Ryles Park County High School

SOMETHING NEW

You ask me what I dreamt?
I dreamt I found something new.
You ask me what I found?
I found a new different computer.
You ask me what it does?
It does what you want it to do.

You ask me what I want?
I want to do something new.
You ask me why I want something new?
I want something new so I can be famous.
You ask my why I want to be famous?
I want to be famous so I will be known everywhere.

You ask me why I want to be known everywhere?
I want to be known everywhere
So that everyone can say 'Hi.'
You ask me why I want everyone to say 'Hi'?
I want them to say 'Hi' so I can say 'Hi' back.
You ask me why I want to say 'Hi'?
I want to say 'Hi' so I can get friends.

Luke Hartley (12)
Ryles Park County High School

HARDCORE ALIEN

He's a hardcore alien from outer space,
He thinks he's cool; he thinks he's ace.
He always comes first in the human race,
He wouldn't settle for second place.

Luke McDonald (12)
Ryles Park County High School

TRAPPED

I wake up all sweaty
You ask me what did I dream?
I was running
From what?
Something.
What?
A creature
What type?
A big creature is what I see.
What did it do?
It was chasing me.
Where?
In the dark.
Where did you go?
Along a dark path.
What happened next?
I saw a pit.
Where did it come from?
I don't know, I ran and ran, not knowing where.
Just a sudden stop.
'No' I screamed, my body banged
against the concrete floor.
My body crumpled all in one,
I scream but nobody hears me.
Trapped is what I feel.
Everything faded back into nothingness.
This is what I dreamt last night.
Trapped.

Linda Phiri (12)
Ryles Park County High School

STARS

Flying in to space was my dream,
opening the shuttle door.
The whoosh of wind in the shuttle.
5, 4, 3, 2, 1, 0, landed.
My heart started to race.
My eyes widened
And I thought to myself.
I will be the first to land on Pluto.
I will be the first to place my foot
on this dodgy, dodgy planet.
To think no one will ever do it
again in this lifetime.
That is what I know, what I will dream
every night when I look at the stars!

Joy King (12)
Ryles Park County High School

BUFFALO SOLDIER

Buffalo Soldier is his name
Grabs machine gun
Takes careful aim.
Head's as big as an elephant's
Holes in his vest
Holes in his pants
Ears as big as paper plates
Tattoos on his arms of poisonous snakes
Cool green hair, spiky with gel
He thinks he's hard, as mean as hell.
Killing aliens every day
You'd better watch out or he'll blow you away.

Liam Alcock (12)
Ryles Park County High School

HAPPY BIRTHDAY LEMONADE

I am sitting in my darkened cell
I look out of the bars.
There I see a party going on
With Starburst, Snickers and Mars.

There I see upon the table
So innocently made
The sweet, sweet liquid on the table
was sweet, sweet lemonade.

In my restraints I couldn't reach
the bottle of lemony goodness.
So I reached out of the bars
and got slapped on the wrist by badness.

I pulled back my arm
in pain and frustration.
I looked at my arm
and looked up with agitation.

I then spun around
and guess what I saw?
An old, old woman
who looked really poor.

I looked in her arms
She was holding a tray
and on this old tray
was my sweet lemonade.

I went for the soda
but to my surprise
I'd then woken up
with dilated eyes.

Simon Mayo (13)
Ryles Park County High School

FLIGHT OF THE ELEPHANT FEAST

As I fly up into the sky,
Many wonders catch my eye.
From pink elephants dancing into their lair,
To colourful fireworks souring into the air.
As I fly, I feel the breeze quite a lot,
Which cools me down as I am too hot!
I feel relaxed and okay,
But then I realise that I haven't eaten all day!
As I fly lower, I start to hear,
Many shouts, laughs and also a cheer.
Then I see a feast, *yes, food!*
That's just what I need to cheer up my mood!
There it is, so nice and hot . . .
Oh no! The greedy elephants have eaten the lot!
I suddenly wake, without eating a crumb . . .
Then there's a *rumble,* it's my tum!

Tom Biggar
Ryles Park County High School

THE WORLD

All the world's a big game
You can go up, down, left or right.
If you go up, you're going on the right path.
If you go down, you're going back on your steps.
If you go left, you're going on the wrong path.
If you go right, you're going back on the right path.
The world is just a big game.
It can be fun, it can be stressful
It can be happy, it can be sad.

Adam Trelfa (12)
Ryles Park County High School

A Bit Of Everything

You asked me what do I dream?
I dream about happiness, love and fear.
You asked me what do I feel?
The truth is I feel emotion, pain and love.
You asked me where my dream is?
My dream is set in places I know and places I don't.
You asked me what do I hear?
I hear horses galloping along a sandy beach
With the tide rolling in and out.
You asked me what I fear?
I fear I get trapped in a dark cave on the beach.
You asked me what do I long for?
I long to be on the horse's back.
You asked me why I have this dream?
Maybe it's because I have my own horse
And love to gallop and know the stable's smell.
Something special anyway.

Sarah Lomas (12)
Ryles Park County High School

Bonfire Night

A hiss of fire fills the air,
A smell of burgers and also smoke,
I love toffee apples and sweets, yum, yum!
The sky is red, green and gold,
As fireworks colour the sky.
'Whiz, bang' go the fireworks
And everybody cheers.

Gareth Maartens (12)
Ryles Park County High School

RIVER OF STRAWBERRY MILKSHAKE

You ask me, what did I dream?
I dreamt that I was on a cliff.
You ask me, why was I on a cliff?
I want to jump off.
You ask me, why do I want to jump off the cliff?
I want to jump into the river of strawberry milkshake
You ask me, river of strawberry milkshake?
Yes, river of cold, thick strawberry milkshake.
You ask me, when am I going to jump into the river?
I jump off the cliff.
You ask me, when am I going to hit the surface?
Now . . . then suddenly the river turns to concrete.
You ask me, am I going to hit the concrete?
I just did.
Then I wake up, face touching the wall.

Christopher Adams (12)
Ryles Park County High School

ROCKET SPINNERS

Fireworks blast off
as they go into the sky
Sparkling colours, *bang!*

As they keep banging
people watch in happiness
red, blue, green and red.

Catherine wheels, rockets
lighting up in the moonlit sky
one catches my sight.

Callum Smythe (11)
Sir Thomas Boteler High School

HALLOWE'EN

Black cats, pumpkins are
Scary in the night, like ghosts,
Witches and white skulls.

Bats and ghosts, screaming
Laughing like witches, loudly,
Children all around.

A witch, a ghost, look real,
But are just costumes,
Children in costumes.

The night is now quiet
There aren't any children
Hallowe'en's finished.

Scott Fisher (11)
Sir Thomas Boteler High School

AUTUMN

Children playing out
Leaves are falling off the trees
They rustle loudly.

Birds in trees tweeting
Sunlight gleaming through the trees
Clouds start to gather.

The rain starts to come
Squirrels go to hide in trees
They gather their nuts.

Bruce McKinnon (12)
Sir Thomas Boteler High School

NATURE

The bottomless sky,
Hustled against misty clouds,
Waiting to make rain.

Mist is dull but grey,
As burnished light crowds the sky,
Plenty of light to gamble.

Reece Hampton (11)
Sir Thomas Boteler High School

POETRY OF AUTUMN

Leaves are falling off
Winds are blowing, cold and soft
Clouds float in the sky
Rivers, they float along.

Fatima Rahman (11)
Sir Thomas Boteler High School

THE BONFIRE

The bonfire hisses
The darkness fills the night sky
Sparkler sparkles bright.

Lauren Himme (11)
Sir Thomas Boteler High School

BONFIRE NIGHT

Big bodacious bangs
from bangers, beautiful,
blown up for big bangs.

Fizzing fireworks
flying through the sky to die
fired from the ground.

Blazing bonfire
enormous and brightly lit
lighting up the dark.

Brian Dickeson (11)
Sir Thomas Boteler High School

LEAVES

Crisp leaves plunge off trees,
twirling madly to the floor,
then they land softly.

Scott Thomas Whitfield (11)
Sir Thomas Boteler High School

FIREWORKS

Autumn is so special
I see fireworks explode,
I like it when the colours glow.

Toby Roy Barnett (11)
Sir Thomas Boteler High School

NATURE IN AUTUMN

Nature is lovely
Owls, bats, squirrels and hedgehogs,
What a sight!

Rustling in the bush
Or even screeching at night
All this in autumn!

Ben Kenyon (11)
Sir Thomas Boteler High School

AUTUMN PONY

On an autumn day
frosty hooves break the silence,
as Jazz canters round.

Galloping wildly,
eyes open, nostrils flaring,
leaves blowing about.

Louise Dack (11)
Sir Thomas Boteler High School

THE HARVEST MOON

Harvest moon shines down
On silver shimmering lakes
Still, deathly water.

Siobhan Davies (12)
Sir Thomas Boteler High School

AUTUMN APPLE

Rosy-red cheeks shine bright,
Swaying in the autumn winds,
Dropping to the ground.

Lying on the leaves,
It sits there like a statue,
Waiting to be found.

Young child finds it,
His eyes sparkle with delight,
Plants it at his house.

Years pass by and still
It grows, healthy as can be.
Soon autumn arrives.

Rosy-red cheeks shine bright,
Swaying in the autumn winds
Dropping to the ground.

Sam Dean (12)
Sir Thomas Boteler High School

ALL HALLOWS EVE

All Hallows Eve's when,
The ghouls come out to play
Darkness rules the night.

As we walk around
Skeletons drop down from trees
While our costumes scare.

James Boucher (11)
Sir Thomas Boteler High School

THE SEA OF LEAVES

Matchbox ships gliding
Across seas of dark large leaves,
Propelled by a gust.

Sea's always growing
The leaves just keep on falling
Into the leaf sea.

Lots of dark colours
Congregating on the road
They just lie there, dead.

Ryan Edwardson (11)
Sir Thomas Boteler High School

HAWK

You are an active theme park
with excitement everywhere I go.
You are an eagle, king of the skies
Controlling your league.

You are sunshine, whatever the weather
You are the sky, you have an everlasting power
Victorious always, never a bad sport
You are loud, but not heavy rock music
entertaining anybody who sees you.

You are life itself
Your are a Mercedes Benz
A shell that attracts an engine which lasts
You are designed to thrill mankind.

Owen Davies (12)
Wilmslow County High School

SCIENTRIFIC!

The start of the lesson
We're in the lab
Pupils are busy at work
Things are going on
I can hear
The scribble of pens
The voice of the teacher
The flame of the Bunsen.

We're watching a video
Things are going on
I can see
The flickering of the television
The colours of pictures
The stillness of the classroom
We're experimenting
Things are going on.

I can smell
The gas of the gas tap
The ink of my pen
The salt in the bowl
There's smoke all around us
There goes the bell.

The lesson is at an end.

Scientrific!

Gemma Connell (11)
Wilmslow County High School

FRIDAY

Start of the day
Waiting in the playground
Then a loud shrill
The bell
I run inside
At my form room I see
A bundle of children chatting away
Another bell
Our tutor lets us in
A calling of names
A bell
A rush to get to the lesson.

'5 x 68' the teacher says
A scribbling of pencils
A scratching of heads
A whisper of voices
A hand shoots up
The answer is said.
A bell
The end of the lesson
The rustling of bags
The zipping of zips
All pile out the door
Break is here.

A munching of food
A shouting of voices
A tweet from the birds
The engine from a train
A bell
A rush for the doors
Next lesson to be had.

A banging of metal
A sawing of saws
A shouting of teachers
The crashing of equipment
Good fun for all
A bell sounds
An urge for food
A dying of thirst
Lunchtime is here

A smell of chips
A murmur of voices
A banging of plates on the table
A splash of water on the floor
A shout for a Miss
They clean it up
Then the bell
The end of lunchtime
One lesson to go.

A yawn from inside
Heads lean on hands
The children are tired
Teachers as well
Then a last bell
A roar of happiness
Home time is here
A charge for the door
A well-earned rest
After a hard week at school

Nick Bazley (11)
Wilmslow County High School

EMMA, YOU ARE . . .

You are a mild sunny day with thin clouds.
You are a sunflower, bright yellow.
You are a cheery, orange umbrella, for wet days.
You are a pair of strappy high heels, for going out.

You can be a gentle stream or an angry waterfall,
You are a cat, a Siamese cat.
You are the summer holidays.

You are a wooden stool,
You are like Eastenders, when it is very dramatic.
But mostly, a bedside lamp.

Alison Jones (12)
Wilmslow County High School

A CACOPHONY OF SOUND

A cacophony of sound as the orchestra tunes,
A blast of the trumpet,
A ting of the triangle,
A flurry of flutes,
A song of a harp,
A screech of a violin,
A twinkle of a flute,
A groan of an oboe,
A roll of a drum,
A clatter of cymbals,
A tap tap of the baton as the music is found.

Sara O'Grady (11)
Wilmslow County High School

A DAY AT SCHOOL

Start of the day
Getting out of the car
Walking to my form room
To have registration
Along the corridor and up the stairs
Rushing by crowds of children
To my form I go
A *bell!* Stop.
Period 1 I go to.

The rushing of children
The stamping of shoes
Into the classroom I go
The ticking of brains
The scratching of pens
In the room is silence
The hands going up
And children asking questions
A *bell!* Stop
Break time is here.

The shouting and pushing
And rushing and running
Crowds of children
Munching away
A *bell!* Stop
Silence broke in
Period 3 I go to.

The silence of reading
No one to disturb
And then silence broke out
'A poem' said our English teacher.

Scott Taylor (11)
Wilmslow County High School

MORNING

The weariness of sleep,
The freshness of a new morning.
The heaviness of tired eyes,
The minty taste of toothpaste,
The splashing of water.
As you wash your face.

The crunching of cornflakes,
The splashing of milk,
The sweetness of sugar,
The buttery toast.

The slam of the door.
The keeping of time,
The rattle of pencils,
Here comes the bus!

The sound of an engine
The grinding of gears,
The natter of children
Ready for school!

Josie Haslam (11)
Wilmslow County High School

LEAH

Leah is the brightest star
The Earth, the sun, the moon.
She is the fluffiest cloud in the sky,
The early birdie's tune.

She is the twinkle in our eyes,
The sun, the wind, the snow.
She's the first snowflake to touch the ground,
And the sweetest person we know

And she isn't gone forever,
She's just having a long, long sleep,
There is no need to say she's gone,
There is no need to weep.

Just because we can't see her,
Doesn't mean she's not near,
So when you're feeling down inside,
We all know she'll always be here.

Sleep tight Leah. XXX

Grace Emily Thorneycroft (11)
Wilmslow County High School

YOU ARE . . .

You are a golden peach,
You are a sunny day,
With thin clouds here and there.
You are the sky,
You stand back and let others shine
You are a blooming rose.

You are spring,
You are a newborn lamb,
You are a sunset,
You are the bark of a tree,
Always there.

You are the first flake of snow,
You are the fresh crisp grass,
You are an old raincoat,
Always protecting others,
You are the view on top of a mountain
Totally unique.

Emma Kerr (12)
Wilmslow County High School

A Day In School

Shuffle of coats
Rush of children
Bash of bags.

Start of the day
Stamping of feet.

Through the gate
A bundle of children
Once again.

Register call
Waiting to work
Working so hard.

New day has begun
Bursting of brains
Ripping of paper.

Try again
The ringing of the bell
The packing of bags.

Through the gate
A bundle of children
Once again.

Register call
Waiting to work
Working so hard.

New day has begun
Bursting of brains
Ripping of paper.

Try again
The ringing of the bell
The packing of bags.

Lunch is here
Frying of chips
Crunching of crisps
Scraping of plates
Rattling of money.

Lunch is over
Sound of music
The ringing of the bell.

Home we go.

Jake Gill (12)
Wilmslow County High School

SAIL

Start of the voyage,
The rising of the sail,
The smell of salt,
The sound of seagulls,
The crunching of pebbles,
As the boat meets the sea.

The feel of solid wood,
The splashing of waves,
The swing of the boom,
The wrench of the main sheet,
The click of the pulleys,
A yell of excitement,

A creak of the rudder,
A crunch of the hull,
As the boat meets solid ground,
The voyage is at an end.

Alex Doherty (11)
Wilmslow County High School

THE SCHOOL DAY

Beginning of the first lesson
The start of the new day
Get out your books
The shuffle of children
The scribbling of pencils
End of the lesson.

Lunch is here
Hundreds of people in a line
The clattering of plates
The sound of children
The munching of food
There's the bell
Back to work.

The curtain ascends
The rehearsal begins
Props are everywhere
Children laugh and shout
Staring at watches
A few boys yawn
Time to go home now
As the day starts to end.

Paul Richardson (11)
Wilmslow County High School

YOU ARE

You are a footballing star
Curling through the defence.
A Porsche starting its engine
A 24 carat gold chain.

You run at the pace of a jaguar
Pouncing on its prey
A heavy metal band
On SMTV Live.

Thomas Larkman (12)
Wilmslow County High School

MUM

You are a warm summer's day,
You are a wonderful homely smell,
You are a pink and peach colour,
and a sweet sounding melody!

You are a big comfy chair,
You are a little thatched cottage,
You are a red, red rose,
the only one there is!

You are an old computer,
definitely not modern,
You are a little star,
guiding me forever!

You are a beach,
though sometimes a meadow,
You are a secret waterfall,
A unique crystal gem!

You are my best friend,
Sometimes,
but most of all you're my mum!

Rachel Moss (12)
Wilmslow County High School

A Day In School

Start of the day
Stamping of feet
Through the gate
A bundle of children
Through the door

                    Register call
                    Waiting to work
                    Working so hard
                    A new day has begun
                    The bursting of brains

Pens at the ready
Oh no!
The ripping of paper
Let's try again
The ringing of the bell.

                    The packing of bags
                    Lunch is here
                    The frying of chips
                    Crunching of crisps
                    Scrapping of plates.

Lunch at an end
Sound of music
Day's at an end.

James Newton (11)
Wilmslow County High School

A Day at School

It's lunch!
The slurping of drinks.
The munching of food,
The hungry people having lunch,
A loud noise,
Sssshhh, be quiet.

Walk down to the field,
Be silent, stay quiet,
Wait 'til we're safe,
At last!

The last lesson,
An end to the day,
We're all tired,
From the things of the day,
We all listen carefully,
To what is said,
With tiredness in our eyes,
Ready to go home,
Ready to relax,
The bell,
Time to go home.

Kathryn Evans (11)
Wilmslow County High School

Sound!

The crash of a drum,
The roar of a plane,
The squeak of a mouse,
Sound is never the same.

It travels in waves,
And bounces off walls,
And echoes around
Empty school halls.

It varies in tempo,
Dynamics and pitch,
As high as the sky,
Or as deep as a ditch.

Loudly or softly,
The decibels ring,
Caused by vibrations,
A squeak or a ping.

Although not as quick,
Or as swift as light,
Sound can keep travelling,
Throughout the night.

Claire Chadwick (14)
Wilmslow County High School

THE BELL

It's the start of the day,
We're arriving at school,
Up to our room,
You're late,
Sorry Sir.

To our next lesson,
The rattle of pencils,
The shuffle of books,
The bell,
Planners out, it's homework.

Out to lunch,
Running and chasing,
Children are happy, but hungry,
The shuffle of coats,
The creak of the chairs,
Children are sitting down to eat.

The bell,
Through the corridors,
To our last lesson,
Children are happy,
Still thinking of the day,
They hear a bell,
And pick up their coats,
Hooray it's home time!

Abby Newell (11)
Wilmslow County High School

A SCHOOL POEM

The sound of the bell!
Teachers shouting your name,
'Yes Sir.'
The bell goes again!
Children shouting
Teachers shouting
'Keep to the left!'
The bell!
'Oh no, I'm lost.'
The teachers showing the way.
Phew, first two periods over.
Break!
The chomping of chocolate
The crunching of crisps
The talking, the football
All in one playground.
The bell!
The third period goes really quickly.
We go to next lesson,
It goes very quickly,
Everybody goes to lunch.
The next two periods go really quickly,
I walk out of the school,
It's the end of the day.

Hayley Williams (11)
Wilmslow County High School

HALLOWE'EN

Yes, it's nearly Hallowe'en
A time when people knock on doors.
It's trick or treat
And you don't know who you will meet.
It's dark, it's cold and it's wet,
But it won't stop me from trick or treating.
Glowing lanterns flickering in windows,
As we pass by
Leaves falling from the trees.
Yes, it's autumn.

John Drinkwater (12)
Wilmslow County High School